The Future of the Automotive Industry

Challenges and Concepts for the 21st Century

Updated Translation

Edited by

Ralf Landmann
Heiko Wolters
Wolfgang Bernhart
Holger Karsten

Arthur D. Little International, Inc.

Society of Automotive Engineers, Inc.
Warrendale, Pa.

Library of Congress Cataloging-in-Publication Data

[Zukunft der Automobilindustrie. English]
   The future of the automotive industry : challenges and concepts for the
21st century : updated translation / edited by Ralf Landmann ... [et al.].
   p. cm.
Includes bibliographical references.
ISBN 0-7680-0688-0
   1. Automobile industry and trade. 2. Automobile industry and trade—
International cooperation. 3. Joint ventures. 4. Globalization. I. Landmann,
Ralf. II. Title.

HD9710.A2 Z85 2000
338.4'76292—dc21   00-045810

Originally published in the German language by Betriebswirtschaftlicher Verlag
Dr. Th. Gabler GmbH, D-65189 Wiesbaden, Germany, under the title "**Heiko Wolters /
Ralf Landmann / Wolfgang Bernhart / Holger Karsten / Arthur D. Little
International (Hrsg.): Die Zukunft der Automobilindustrie** 1. Auflage 1999."
© by Gabler Verlag GmbH, Wiesbaden, 1999.

Updated translation Copyright © 2001

                        Society of Automotive Engineers, Inc.
                        400 Commonwealth Drive
                        Warrendale, PA 15096-0001 U.S.A.
                        Phone: (724) 776-4841 • Fax: (724) 776-5760
                        E-mail: publications@sae.org
                        http://www.sae.org

ISBN 0-7680-0688-0

SAE Order No. R-291

Contents

Preface

Since its publication in autumn 1998, the German edition of *The Future of the Automotive Industry* established itself as a profound reference for automotive executives among car and truck manufacturers, suppliers, and automotive service providers.

We believe that every automotive company has the opportunity to proactively shape its own future. This requires not only a sound and clear understanding of current reality and future developments, but also the courage to move beyond incrementalism to create an exciting new horizon of opportunities. Old recipes from the drawer won't work—fresh and innovative ideas are required to unleash the potential of each company.

This book resulted from our daily consulting work with industry leaders world-wide. It provides the ideas, concepts, and tools to shape your part of the automotive world—without pretending to have patent solutions for every issue. No one will revolutionize the automotive industry merely by reading a book. However, the examples provided here could improve your odds of developing and implementing a winning strategy. We would like to encourage you to do just that.

We thank all of our colleagues at Arthur D. Little, especially Verena Lau and Ashok Boghani for making this book possible and for coping with the logistics of writing a book from several points around the globe.

Ralf Landmann, Heiko Wolters, Wolfgang Bernhart, Holger Karsten
Arthur D. Little International, Inc.
Wiesbaden, Germany/Cambridge, Massachusetts
March 2000

What Challenges Face the Automobile Industry?

Tom Sommerlatte, Holger Karsten

In 1996, the automobile industry celebrated its 100th anniversary. Over these 100 years, annual production developed from the coach-like motor vehicles of Carl Benz to approximately 50 million state-of-the-art vehicles, and the number of motorized vehicles (cars and trucks) has increased to nearly 500 million units worldwide today. The year 2000 is marked by the entire industry's efforts to embrace e-business—to get the car into the Web and the Web into the car.

Tremendous developments took place in all areas of the automobile industry: performance, fuel consumption, safety, comfort, and information for the driver. Fuel consumption has been reduced while keeping the same performance or even improving it, and prices have fallen in relation to the features and quality of the vehicles. We already see the first vehicles that can exchange information via modern communication systems and the Internet, taking the strain off the driver in a number of situations. Routes can be optimized, taking into account traffic situations, and garages can be notified of any preventive maintenance work without the vehicle owner having to think of it himself.

At the same time, manufacturers and suppliers have optimized internal structures and processes, achieving enormous improvements in efficiency. Between 1986 and 1996, for example, Volkswagen increased the number of vehicles produced per employee by nearly 50 percent.

At first sight, it would appear that we are experiencing a successful start into the new millennium. However, if we look more closely, a number of crucial questions pose a great challenge for everyone concerned:

- How will demand shift between "mature" markets and emerging regions such as Eastern Europe, China, and South America? How should motor vehicle manufacturers and suppliers react to the accelerating trend toward globalization? Or have we already surpassed the peak?

- What effect will growing concentration have on the competitive structure of the motor vehicle and supplier industries?

- How can OEMs and suppliers master technological innovation in the years to come or even shape it?

- How will increasing environmental demands affect products and production?

- What opportunities does information technology offer? For what changes should dealers, manufacturers, and suppliers prepare in their core processes—beyond the dot.com hype?

Many more questions could be added to this list—their implied challenges alone must be taken into account in any strategy that is developed. Demand in the established triad markets will remain low, despite the marked recovery from the recession in the early 1990s. In 2003, we can expect a market volume of approximately 18.1 million units in North America and approximately 15.7 million units in Europe. However, these levels were already reached in 1987.

Manufacturers in the established (motor vehicle) countries will have to counter the generally weak growth in demand with products designed to meet specific requirements of individual customer groups. The growing trend toward segmentation into ever smaller customer groups has led to a greater variety of models. If manufacturers and suppliers are to cope with this complexity, they will have to adapt their products (platform or module design concepts) and processes (development, supply chain management, and marketing/distribution). Moreover, many more customer segments must be addressed individually. It is the task of manufacturers to find a suitable strategy to manage these multimarkets.

Changes in the demographic structure as well as in values are reinforcing this trend toward more individualized products. Customers in the mature markets will no longer be satisfied by owning only one vehicle, but may want to use (not necessarily buy) the most suitable vehicle for each specific activity: a jeep for a short trip to the mountains, a convertible in the summer, and a saloon with all-wheel drive in the winter season. This vision of a different "transportation agent" depending on the season or activity has already been embraced by some innovative leasing companies. In the area of service, customized offerings based on standardized modules are becoming more and more popular. The keywords for the future are "choice" and "flexibility."

Suppliers will have to follow the OEMs. Size is a vital factor in the struggle for survival if the suppliers are to develop the required competencies. The large number of acquisitions and joint ventures in the supply industry speak the language of globalization. The demands placed on the suppliers are mani- fold. They must find their optimum position in the value chain, develop a feasible globalization strategy, set priorities in the innovation process, optimize their own processes, and also ensure knowledge transfer on a global level— all under the umbrella of global e-procurement and emering B2B-enchanges.

In addition to globalization, customer behavior, and price pressure, technology also plays a crucial role in shaping the structure of the industry. Recent years have seen great benefits for car users as a result of advances in electric and electronic technology. Many more developments will follow, especially those designed to simplify the complexity of operations and handling. The Internet has become a part of daily life, reaching out and into the car. Virtually every conceivable area will be affected, be it in the form of a communication medium between driver and service point, new electronic markets for potential buyers, sales channels that will be powerful competitors for the traditional dealers, or a medium for communication with suppliers.

However, it is not enough to only be aware of the problems and challenges of the future. Solutions are needed—not in the form of magic formulas, but as feasible and practicable approaches. In this book, clients and consult- ants of Arthur D. Little's Global Automotive Practice present tested and proven concepts. These contributions are described from the viewpoints of OEMs, suppliers, and trade. We have supplemented them with our know- how, acquired in many projects on which we have worked around the world. The following chapters portray in detail the most important factors influenc- ing the development of the automobile industry, and they outline approaches to meet these challenges.

On the Way to Globalization— Opportunities and Risks

Heiko Wolters, Sylvia Enders[1]

> *It is not enough to know; you must make use of it.*
> *It is not enough to want; you must do it as well.*
> —Johann Wolfgang von Goethe

While the triad markets of Western Europe, North America, and Japan are characterized by increased competition, high local costs, and market saturation, regions such as South America, Asia, or Eastern Europe promise high future growth potential for the automobile industry.

This development has led many car manufacturers to position themselves more globally in the market. High import duties and import restrictions often make it impossible to penetrate the growth regions with strategies relying purely on exports from plants in the home country. Local production with a considerable share of local content, in addition to an adequate sales and service network, are needed to achieve significant market share.

The automotive supplier industry must adapt to the globalization of its customers as well. Considering the developments toward worldwide platforms and global sourcing strategies, parts supply companies are required to be present locally at the production sites of their OEM customers. In addition, the local supplier base in the target regions of the vehicle manufacturers is often underdeveloped, so that the supplier who follows his customer abroad is often a welcome source of supply for local OEMs as well.

---

1 The authors thank Ralf Hocke for valuable contributions.

In this chapter, the subject of globalization is treated in two sections. The first section explains the strategic importance of globalization. The second section deals with the operative implementation of a globalization project.

The Strategic Importance of Globalization

The decision to become a "global" organization is not merely limited to additional sales potential. Globalization is a complex venture based on many factors. The following are among the most important ones.

Exploiting the Opportunities for Growth

In 1998, 37.4 million passenger vehicles were sold worldwide. Of these, 27.3 million vehicles were sold in the countries of Western Europe, North America, and Japan. With a world market share of 73 percent, the triad markets are therefore the most important sales regions. A worldwide volume of 41.3 million vehicles is estimated for the year 2003. Sales in the triad countries are anticipated at 28.1 million units, amounting to a world market share of 68 percent. This means that the classic automobile markets will remain the most important sales targets in the future.

Another picture emerges if you examine the growth rates in the triad countries for the period 1998 to 2003. Europe and Japan achieve an annual growth rate of less than 1 percent. The original pessimistic forecast for the U.S. market (an annual decline of 0.6 percent per year) has been proven incorrect after a spectacular market growth in 1999 and the rapid start of 2000. However, this growth still does not match the expectations for the markets in Eastern Europe, South America, and Asia (Japan excluded), which are estimated to grow at 7.9, 7.7, and 7.5 percent, respectively. All in all, the world market share of these emerging markets will increase from 20 to 25 percent, and the sales volume will grow from 7.4 million to 10.4 million units (Fig. 1).

The predictions show that the established markets in Western Europe, North America, and Japan will continue to be the most important sales markets in terms of volume. However, no growth is expected in these regions. Therefore, increases in market share will be possible only by replacing existing competitors.

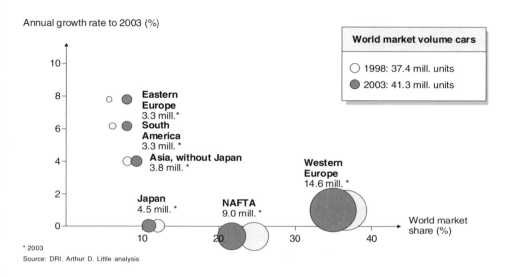

Annual growth rate to 2003 (%)

* 2003

Source: DRI. Arthur D. Little analysis

Figure 1   Sales potential by region.

On the other hand, through geographic expansion in the markets in Eastern Europe, South America, or Asia, the car OEMs and their suppliers can exploit growth opportunities. Furthermore, they can build barriers to entry for competitors through early entrance into these markets.

Reducing Unit Costs and Increasing Profitability

Sales in a new market increase the total sales per product. This allows higher economies of scale along the value chain and reduces the cost per vehicle. Research and development costs are distributed across more units per model, and purchasing obtains lower prices per component through the greater purchase volume from global sourcing contracts. Productivity gains in production are achieved through increased output due to learning effects. In planning for the Mercedes A Class, for example, production in South America was included in the calculations from the beginning. In addition, research and development costs could be distributed across a much greater vehicle volume, which reduced the calculated costs per vehicle.

In addition to high corporate tax rates and capital costs, wages and nonwage labor costs burden the cost structures in the industrialized countries. By shifting production to countries with low location costs, considerable savings can be achieved. The preferred target countries for Western European car makers are currently Poland, the Czech Republic, and Hungary. These countries combine comparatively low location cost with highly qualified and motivated personnel. Audi made the decision to assemble its new TT sport coupe in Györ in Hungary for this reason. Looking at the German automobile industry as a whole, this trend is confirmed. In the 1980s, only 23 percent of the total production by German manufacturers came from foreign production sites; however, by 1998, it had already reached 37 percent.

Protecting the Home Markets

The presence of the most important competitors in the home markets indirectly protects one's own home market when the products compete with each other. This results from the fact that the market prices can no longer be seen as singular for a section of the market, but for all markets together. If the foreign competitor is also present in the home market and vice versa, destabilizing strategies by individual market participants (e.g., price dumping) are prevented.

Balancing Economic Fluctuations and Exchange Rate Risks

The expansion of activities into new regions means that sales development no longer depends exclusively on the economic development of the home market. Because economic cycles usually differ across regions, recessive symptoms in one country can be balanced in another market. Furthermore, a harmonized network of locations reduces exchange rate risks. Thus, for example, Toyota was profitable in spite of the recession in Asia in 1997/1998 because the profits from its production sites in North America and Europe offset the poor results in Asia.

Gaining Market Share Through Local Production

Studies have shown that the degree of recognition and the loyalty of customers to a specific manufacturer increases significantly through local assembly and production, and that the manufacturer subsequently gains market share. Loyalty effects with which the local economy is strengthened cause this phenomenon. Sometimes, this effect is even promoted by national legal requirements. Thus, for example, in the United States, there are labeling regulations for vehicles according to which both the proportion of parts from the United States and Canada, as well as the place of final assembly, must be listed.

Suppliers Will Have to Follow Their Customers

The necessity to follow customers results from the strategy of the vehicle manufacturers to use only one worldwide supplier for platforms and models. In addition, suitable suppliers for complex systems may not be easy to find in developing countries. This makes the global presence of the parts suppliers a selection criterion when awarding supply volumes. If the suppliers cannot meet these demands, losses of contracts could ensue also in the home markets. In addition to increased sales to existing customers, commitment abroad allows the opportunity to acquire new local customers.

Overcapacities and Financial Risks

The aforementioned advantages are counterbalanced by various risks. A global engagement can become a problem when the planned activities abroad do not adequately consider competitors' activities, resulting in overcapacities in the regions initially judged attractive. If, for example, all of the plants currently being planned for South America are actually built, capacities will have doubled by the year 2001. Because demand will not increase to the same extent in this region during the next few years, a reduced capacity utilization rate is to be expected for the vehicle manufacturers. Thus, the decision to enter into a new market must not be completely detached from the strategies of the competition.

Furthermore, unexpected economic fluctuations, social unrest, or changes in the political structure can adversely affect an engagement abroad, with the consequence that the expected payback comes at a time much later than originally planned. Companies having invested in Brazil, for example, currently suffer from an economic downturn with lower vehicle demand than originally forecasted.

Direction of Globalization

The question as to what degree of globalization must be achieved is not an easy one to answer. The decision depends on the role of the company within the automotive industry. Considering manufacturers, entry into new markets depends largely on the market segments covered. A maker of economical compact cars will establish production in low-wage countries such as India or China before the maker of a luxury car would do so. The path to globalization on the part of suppliers depends greatly on their position within the supplier pyramid. Systems suppliers that deliver complete modules will enter foreign markets before parts suppliers that fear stronger local competition and have fewer opportunities to differentiate themselves from the competition.

The question as to which region or country a company should move into for globalization must be answered individually. The decision depends on the product range, the current degree of globalization, the cost structure, the financial strength, and the management resources of the company in question. In addition to the established markets, which are interesting expansion targets because of their size, the growth regions of South America, Asia, and Eastern Europe are becoming more popular. In the year 2003, one-quarter of the world production will be sold in these markets. To identify the target country within the "new" markets, the regions must be examined carefully. Today, the greatest growth in Asia appears to be centered in India, China, and the ASEAN economic block. In Eastern Europe, the greatest growth potential is in Russia, as well as in the next group of candidates for EU membership: Poland, the Czech Republic, and Hungary. In South America, two economic blocks exist: (1) the Mercosur, with the member states of Brazil, Argentina, Paraguay, and Uruguay, and (2) the Andes Pact, with the member states of Bolivia, Columbia, Ecuador, Peru, and Venezuela. A brief characterization of the growth markets is depicted in Fig. 2.

Growth Region South America

While many countries in Asia and Eastern Europe are only at the beginning of their economic development, some countries in South America already have markets of significant size. In Brazil, for example, more new vehicles were sold in 1998 than in all other South American countries combined. Growth also can be expected for the future. The Brazilian market will grow annually

Region / Criteria	South America		Asia			Eastern Europe	
	Mercosur	Andes Pact	ASEAN	China	India	EU member candidates[2]	Russia
Population ('98 in mill.)	208	106	506	1,239	980	59	146
GDP ('98 in bill. US-$)	1,107	277	514	961	397	260	275
GDP growth ('96 - '98 p.a.)	1.3%	6.4%	2.7%	8.7%	4.2%	4.9	- 4%
GDP per capita ('98)	5,331	2,614	1,015	770	406	4,406	1,884
Vehicle density, cars[1] ('97)	90	35	17	4	4	222	90
Market development car sales '97 - '03 (in mill. units)							

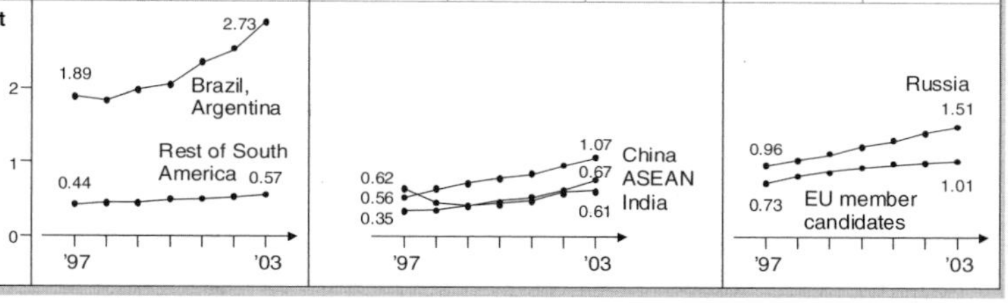

Source: Statistisc Rundesant VDA DRI Arthur D. Little analysis   1) Vehicles per 1,000 inhabitants   2) Poland, Hungary, Czech Republic

Figure 2   Brief characterization of growth markets.

at a rate of 5.3 percent until the year 2003, and the entire region at a rate of 6.2 percent. In 2003, as many vehicles will be sold in Brazil as will be sold in France. Likewise, the South American market will become almost as important as the German one, with sales of 3.3 million units in 2003.

This development is promoted by the planned creation of a common economic area without trade barriers. By the year 2000, this should have been accomplished among the Mercosur member states. By the year 2005, an integration of the member states of the Andes Pact is planned.

The auto manufacturers currently have capacities of 2.5 million units annually in South America. By the year 2001, capacity will have almost doubled to 4.6 million units. DaimlerChrysler, for example, recently introduced the A Class in Juiz de Fora, and Audi introduced the A3 in Curitiba. The increase in capacity on the side of the manufacturers makes the South American market much more attractive to smaller supplier firms because the sales potential for many suppliers has already reached the necessary minimum size and justifies local production. However, companies wishing to expand in this region will have to hurry if they want to position themselves in the market in time.

Growth Region Asia

Although the effects of the Asian crisis will continue to be felt in large parts of the region during the next few years, this continent will be the center of growth in the 21st century, with the enormous market potential of India and China. A glance at the planned investment volumes of the car OEMs confirms this estimate: vehicle manufacturers plan to invest 16 billion U.S. dollars in new production sites in Asia. This is equivalent to half of the planned investments in the three growth regions of South America, Eastern Europe, and Asia.

India and China, with more than two billion inhabitants, offer enormous market potential. With Gross Domestic Product growth rates of 4 and 8.7 percent, respectively, between 1996 and 1998, both nations have an economic growth that is above average. Which path of economic development both nations will take in the future depends greatly on political stability and development. In China, future growth especially depends on the readiness of the political leadership to open up to the world to a greater extent and to introduce the structures of a market economy. India remains divided by massive social and religious differences, 50 years after independence from Great Britain.

In the medium term (i.e., by 2003), China is expected to double its market volume to more than one million passenger vehicles. In India, sales are expected to increase between 1997 and 2003 by 10 percent annually to more than 600,000 units.

Although the automobile industry and major suppliers are including India and China more and more in their investment plans, the question for small companies increasingly is the time at which they should enter the market. The optimal moment for an entry in India or China can be determined only by each individual company. However, the planning should consider that both markets are in the early stages of development. In China, for example, enough time for negotiations with the government must be included in the planning.

In addition to Korea and Japan, the Asian crisis has especially affected the ASEAN member states. The car markets in Indonesia, Thailand, Malaysia, and the Philippines collapsed in 1997 and will slowly recover in the coming years. In the medium to long term, the chances for Asia to overcome the current turbulence are rather good. The basic conditions for the sale of automobiles continue to be positive in the ASEAN countries. If we examine the density of vehicles as an indicator of potential vehicle sales, there remains an enormous need to catch up to the level of industrialized countries. For example, every other person in Germany owns a car; however, in Thailand, only every eleventh inhabitant does.

Politics is also showing signs of continuing the course of economic integration in spite of the current problems. The governments of the member states agreed on an accelerated plan for the formation of the Asian Free Trade Area (AFTA). By the year 2003, rather than the year 2008 as originally planned, the tariff and non-tariff trade barriers among the member states will be eliminated, and a common economic area will be created.

For the Western automotive industry, the economic turbulence in the region offers a historic opportunity to build a good competitive position in the ASEAN area in the short term and therefore to participate in future growth. The massive devaluation of the local currencies, the readiness of many governments to promote foreign investment with attractive incentives, and the liquidity bottlenecks of many local companies currently make possible a comparatively inexpensive entry into the market.

Growth Region Eastern Europe

Similar to Asia, the region of Eastern European countries must be examined individually. While the EU membership candidates Poland, Hungary, and the Czech Republic are at the beginning of an economic catch-up process comparable to that of Greece, Spain, and Portugal in the 1980s, the other Eastern European countries are developing very differently. Countries such as Croatia, Latvia, or Slovakia are trying hard to prepare for candidacy for EU membership; however, the situation concerning reforms is uncertain in other countries, especially in Russia, the Ukraine, and White Russia. The Gross Domestic Product in Poland, Hungary, and the Czech Republic grew by 4.9 percent annually between 1996 and 1998, while the Gross Domestic

Product in Russia declined by 2.1 percent. Nevertheless, an increase in car sales volume from 1 million to 1.5 million is estimated by the year 2003. In the three EU membership candidates, the passenger car market will increase by 39 percent between 1997 and 2003, and sales volume then will achieve more than 1 million units. In addition to the sales potential, Eastern Europe is attractive to many automobile manufacturers and suppliers as a production site because the region has qualified personnel at wages that are relatively low in comparison to those in the industrialized nations. Likewise, it is located geographically close to Western Europe.

The Implementation of Globalization

The analysis of possible target regions is one of the major bases of globalization considerations. To utilize all of the advantages of globalization mentioned, the theoretical venture must turn into concrete action. A four-step process has proven to be successful in numerous projects undertaken by Arthur D. Little (Fig. 3).

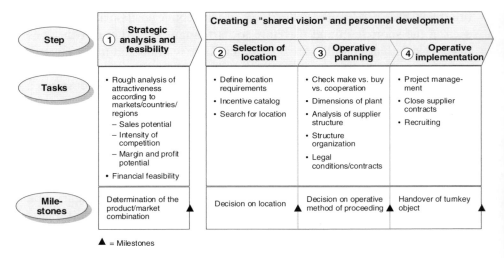

Figure 3   Step-by-step plan for globalization.

The basis for the decision is the strategic analysis as well as the feasibility. In this step, the markets in question are evaluated with respect to sales potential and competitive intensity, as well as the strategic direction of the company. In addition, the achievable margins and the profit potential should be estimated. Building on this is the determination of the product-market combination to be pursued. This outlines the geographic direction of the globalization plan.

In the second step, the location is selected. To make a decision on the location, the essential requirements of the location must be defined, and possible sites must be evaluated accordingly.

The operative planning, the third step, includes questions of internal versus external production and internal organization.

In the fourth step, the operative implementation of operation up to the handover of the turnkey object takes place. The following section describes the first three steps in more detail.

Strategic Analysis and Feasibility

Because the foreign branch of a company often has to cover several areas in a region, the selection of the country must be considered carefully. Thus, possible destination countries should be evaluated using various criteria to determine the general strategy and feasibility:

- Market attractiveness in terms of unit volume of the product as well as market growth

- Competitive intensity: The danger of the market entry of new competitors, rivalry among existing competitors, power of the suppliers and customers, danger of product substitution

- Political and economic stability of the country: The development of the politically active forces and the majority relationships in the parliament and population, long-term political consequences in case the power changes, the future direction of economic policy and reforms

- Image of the country for the company: The future effect of the image of a foreign production location on the product and the brand, attributes of each nation's industry in comparison to the brand (e.g., with respect to quality of workmanship, life expectancy, or stability of values)

- Infrastructure, logistics, communication: The availability of communications facilities, roads, railway lines, airports, and seaports; availability and quality of services

- Supplier structure and assurance of supply: The development of the number and structure of the local suppliers, and the willingness of existing suppliers to local engagement

- Personnel qualifications and availability: The level of education; the necessary qualification measures, development of the availability and quality of the potential labor force

- Opportunity to open additional new markets: Economic relations with other countries as part of free trade areas, international economic promotion

- Regulations by government and employee representatives: Economic and environmental regulations (e.g., local content regulations and license regulations), evaluation of the power of and the cooperation with employee representatives

Special country reports can be used to acquire data for the analysis of these criteria. For example, on the Internet, the European Community offers its Market Access Database (http://mkaccdb.eu.int). Likewise, the Office of Automotive Affairs of the U.S. Department of Commerce (http://ita.doc.gov) offers extensive information on the automobile industry by country. It contains, for example, information on investment and import guidelines, and tariff and non-tariff barriers to trade. The corresponding chambers of commerce or national statistical offices also often have extensive information on selected countries.

Beyond that, special institutes can perform risk evaluations, such as the BERI Index (Business Environment Risk Index), which can be useful in selecting a country. The degree of risk for approximately 50 countries is evaluated, based on the operative risk (stability of macroeconomic factors), the political risk (political and social conditions), and the ability to return capital. In addition, recommendations on quality of investment (profit opportunity recommendations) are made for each country. These recommendations, however, can serve only as a guideline because the information on which the evaluation is based is not published.

After the countries in consideration have been analyzed and evaluated according to these criteria, the countries are prioritized according to their usefulness. This is done by evaluating the relative advantages of locating in target countries, using weighted total scores. This examination of usefulness is especially good for complex evaluations; a structured approach is essential when a number of criteria must be considered.

Finding the Right Location

After the country of location has been decided, possible locations within the country should be evaluated. Because the selection of the location is an extraordinarily complex undertaking, it is a good idea to tackle the decision in several steps in which the selection criteria are refined gradually (Fig. 4).

In the first step, the minimum requirements that the location must fulfill are considered. Not more than five to ten criteria should be used here, and they should eliminate some potential locations. This could, for example, be climatic conditions, distances to commercial locations (e.g., airports, seaports), energy connections, or the level of education. Experience has shown that the number of potential regions can be reduced by 50 percent in this way.

The second step evaluates the remaining regions based on 20 to 30 regional criteria, which must cover social, demographic, and infrastructure aspects. These may be, for example, population and growth, per capita Gross Domestic Product, or the labor force potential. Only about 20 percent of the regions initially examined typically pass this filter.

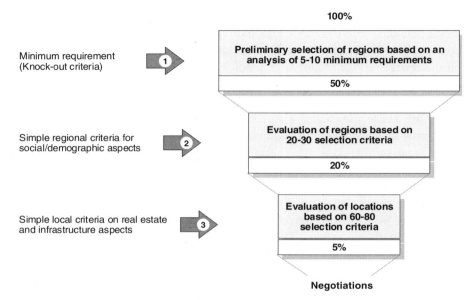

Figure 4   Location selection filter.

In the third step, the potential locations within the regions selected are analyzed using 60 to 80 local criteria. Examples of location criteria are:

- Entrepreneurial climate in the locations
- Quality of the land to be acquired
- Regulations and approvals
- Traffic connections
- Supply and waste disposal
- Communication
- Labor market potential
- Opportunities for further and continuing education
- Quality of life

These criteria also should be refined and evaluated for each potential location. Thus, for example, the criteria "geological base data" can be described by the area, emissions, topography, boundary lines, seismic data, type of soil, ability to bear a load, contamination of the soil, or groundwater conditions.

Case Study:
The Search for a Location for Brose Fahrzeugteile GmbH & Co.
KG, Coburg, Germany

In 1998, Brose set a goal of becoming a global player in South America with its own production site. As a supplier of door modules for the Volkswagen Golf A4 and the Volkswagen Passat B5, as well as of window lifters and seat adjustment systems for the Mercedes A Class in Germany, it also had the opportunity to supply to both customers locally. As a result of the economic downturn, the A Class is currently assembled in quantities of approximately 25,000 units per year in the Mercedes plant in Juiz de Fora, although the capacity is almost 100,000. The Volkswagen Group has built the Audi A3 in Curitiba since 1999 and the Golf A4 in another plant in Brazil. A subcompact car will follow in 2002.

Brose calculated a time period of 14 months until the production plant would be ready for handover. Based on the delivery of the door modules using just-in-time logistics, it quickly became clear that a location in the immediate vicinity of the Volkswagen plant in Curitiba had to be found. When searching for the site, the following criteria were used:

- Distance to the Volkswagen plant <10 km

- Travel time to ensure just-in-time delivery: maximum 20 minutes

- Minimum size of the property of 30,000 m^2, with a possible expansion of 15,000 m^2

- No limitations on buildings

- No pollution problems from the past (expert report)

- Length-to-width ratio of 1:1.5 to 1:2

- Load-bearing ability of the ground at least 200 kN/m^2

Locations in the industrial park next to the Volkswagen plant were rejected because of the small size of the lots and the lack of space for future expansion. Instead, a piece of property used agriculturally in the immediate vicinity of the customer (distance of approximately 2 km) was bought; however, the property had to be rezoned for industrial development. After building the factory by the end of 1998, production started in the spring of 1999. In total, 13 million U.S. dollars were invested for the building and property.

Local chambers of commerce are a source for finding potential locations, as are real estate agents or communities. Frequently, regional governments even have special offices that can advise and help potential investors. If a supplier is following a vehicle manufacturer, it is worthwhile to see if a supplier park is planned in the immediate vicinity of the manufacturer's assembly plant.

Every location under consideration should then be subjected to a benefit analysis. Only the best-ranked locations should be further pursued in a later round—for example, as part of the incentive negotiations with the local officials. Extensive incentives should be the subject of negotiations with the responsible authorities, not only in developing and newly industrialized countries, but also in industrialized regions. However, it must be determined who is the authorized partner for the negotiation of incentives because the responsibility may lie at a local level in one case and at a national level in another.

With regard to incentives, a general differentiation must be made between the basic fiscal and monetary incentives. Fiscal incentives refer to liberation from or reduction of community fees, reductions in value added or income taxes, or the ability to transfer losses among affiliated companies. The monetary incentives include, among other things, financial benefits from low interest rates and favorable deadlines; payment in kind in the form of property, buildings, or electricity; gas and water connections; and taking qualification measures for the employees or infrastructure projects. Frequently, entire services, such as the qualification of future employees or providing transportation for employees to and from the plant, is undertaken by the authorities.

The extent of the possible incentives depends on the planned investment sum. Thus, large companies with extensive projects have a better negotiating position than mid-sized companies with relatively small investments. Furthermore, the attractiveness of the local region can influence the incentives. Thus, in structurally weak regions, incentives of up to 75 percent of the total investment sum are possible. Simultaneously, legal experts should be consulted to examine the legal validity of promises made by the authorities.

Operations Planning

In any globalization plan, the decision must be made regarding whether activities abroad are to be initiated alone or with a partner, and which ventures are to be launched alone and which require help from others. Although country-specific peculiarities have a significant influence on this decision, the make-or-buy strategy should be developed in alignment with the company and business sector strategies.

The low investments, the ability to have variable costs, the reduction of complexity, and the greater flexibility all favor the decision to buy. Internal production is preferred, especially when control of important technologies, assurance of quality, and avoidance of dependence are important parameters in making the decision.

However, make-or-buy decisions are rarely "either/or" decisions. Depending on the intensity of the cooperation, numerous forms of cooperation can be found, such as joint ventures or alliances. A decision matrix with the parameters "need for coordination" and "abilities in comparison to the competition" can be helpful in narrowing the form of cooperation (Fig. 5).

If entry into the destination country will be implemented with a partner, several opportunities for cooperation with other companies up to and including acquisition should be examined. Cooperation can be advantageous, especially when the partner knows the local customs in dealing with the authorities, customers, or unions. This solution should be considered seriously when entering new markets in which your company has no experience in doing business. Furthermore, the cooperating partner can generate interesting synergies between your own resources and its facilities, customers, employees, or know-how.

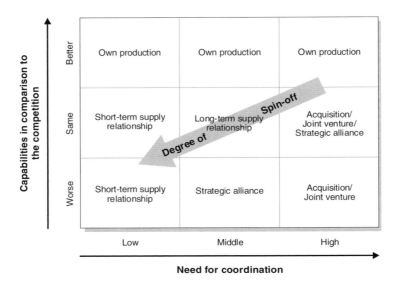

Figure 5 Make-or-buy or cooperation.

If cooperation with a partner is desired, then possible candidates should be evaluated in a three-step process. In this process, various filters should be used to continually reduce the number of potential partners:

- Filter 1 (Screening Criteria): The compatibility of possible companies is evaluated on the basis of desk research; that is, data such as product groups, turnover, profits, customer base, or production sites.

- Filter 2 (Ranking Criteria): Companies are evaluated according to their quality, competencies in development, production, logistics, technological know-how, and management.

- Filter 3 (Selection Criteria): Detailed analysis of selected candidates with reference to strategic fit and potential synergies, cultural fit, company value, innovation climate, legal security from patents, registered trademarks, etc.

However, the possible advantages and the design of a cooperation solution (e.g., with respect to the extent of capital involvement) must be critically examined.

A hurriedly created cooperation can become a burden for the company's own development when the initial hurdles have been overcome. The most common mistakes that lead to the failure of cooperations are an inadequate analysis of the stand-alone perspectives and possible synergies in the negotiation phase, and an inadequate integration of the partner after conclusion of the cooperation agreement. Frequently, the differing cultures, unwritten rules, and a lack of consensus within the management split the cooperating companies.

In addition to the proportion manufactured by oneself and by others, the structural organization is an important factor in the operation planning of any globalization effort. This includes not only the organization of the operation abroad but also its integration in the parent company.

The resulting globalization is characterized by regional locations that are equal partners, existing side by side and jointly contributing to the financial and technological results of the group worldwide. Products in this scenario are manufactured as a global platform with local adjustments. The business processes are globally integrated, while the comparative advantages of the different locations are utilized.

This requires that the locations are not thought of merely as satellites of the headquarters; rather, a process of synchronization and integration is implemented, with the goal of exhausting more completely the market and technology opportunities. This also requires an information technology link among the units to ensure that knowledge can be exchanged among locations.

Globalization—*Quo vadis?*

Neither today nor in the future must automobile manufacturers or their suppliers be globally present without a comprehensive sales and service network and local production. The decision on the optimal degree of globalization and the regional portfolio must be made individually for each company. This decision depends primarily on what role the company plays in the automotive industry and what products the company manufactures, as well as on the know-how and size of the company.

Successful entry into a new market also depends on timing. If the selected location is built too early, the project may fail in spite of high growth expectations. On the other hand, a latecomer in attractive regions may find a situation in which the barriers to entry created by the now-established competitors are too high, meaning that the engagement abroad should have been completed earlier.

Projects by Arthur D. Little show that a few parameters determine the success of a globalization plan. A carefully detailed analysis of the strategic starting point and the strategic options should be the basis of any globalization plan.

- The business plan should define explicitly the path of development for the operation abroad. It should include the markets and the potential customers, as well as the precise volume to be sold.

- The globalization plan should work within a defined time schedule, based on milestones that prioritize the goals to be achieved.

- A balance between central control and local autonomy should be achieved, based on clear and balanced guidelines that take into account the decision-making competencies, e.g., the determination of product concepts, technical standards, make-or-buy decisions, or capital investments.

- Qualified personnel represent a critical bottleneck resource in every company. Both the selection of suitable personnel, as well as the preparation of existing personnel, for the assignment abroad should be given adequate time and attention in advance.

Literature

Funakawa, S., and Funakawa, A., *Transcultural Management: A New Approach for Global Organizations*, Jossey-Bass Business & Management Series, San Francisco, CA, 1997.

Kanter, R.M., *World Class: Thriving Locally in the Global Economy*, Simon & Schuster, New York, NY, 1997.

Shimokawa, K., "Restructuring and Global Strategy of Japanese Automobile Industry and Its Perspective," International Motor Vehicle Program Research Paper, Massachusetts Institute of Technology, Cambridge, MA, 1995.

Standard & Poor's DRI: World Car Industry Forecast Report, May 1998, Lexington, MA.

The Brazilian Automotive Industry— Historic and Future Perspectives

Marcos Chiorboli, Christian Orglmeister

The Starting Challenge

The automotive industry in Brazil began in the 1920s with Ford's CKD vehicles assembly line in São Paulo, with the parts coming directly from the United States. In an effort to industrialize the country, the government provided incentives for the installation of new factories. This permitted multinational companies such as Ford, GM, Fiat, Volkswagen, and Willys Overland to own 100 percent of the equity in their Brazilian operations. Some Brazilian-owned companies also were created, such as Vemag (Veículos e Máquinas Agrícolas) and state-owned FNM (Fábrica Nacional de Motores).

Next, the import of FBU (fully built unit) vehicles was allowed. However, over-taxation impacted the profile of cars being produced in the country. Thus, the most sophisticated models were imported, whereas local production focused on low-price models. However, the government insisted that the companies quickly convert from those building from kits of imported parts to those that use practically 100 percent local content parts. This was intended to spur the development of a domestic auto parts industry.

By the mid-1960s, the government restricted the import of FBUs, resulting in the change of the production profile. The production of larger and more sophisticated vehicles had started. At the same time, industry began changing through acquisitions and new entrants. For example, Volkswagen acquired Vemag, Ford acquired Willys, and Chrysler started operations in Brazil.

In the 1970s, the import of FBUs was prohibited. This forced the OEMs installed in the country to produce a greater range of products than in the past, in order to maximize local content investments. Demand was growing, with the Brazilian average annual growth rate at a high 7 percent throughout the 1970s. In the midst of the Brazilian economic miracle, the Brazilian industry produced 1 million units annually. In this buoyant scenario, Fiat do Brasil started local production of its 147 model by 1975.

The year 1980 set a turning point for the industry. The "Lost Decade" was ready to begin: a long period of stagnation and economic instability. As noted, the mass-production complexes built in Brazil were a notable achievement compared with the alternative of complete dependence on imports. However, these plants lagged far behind those in other parts of the world in terms of productivity and product quality. Because of legal restrictions on the import of computers and microprocessors, several technological devices that appeared in OEM headquarters were not incorporated into the local production. In addition, the world oil crises in the early 1970s led the government to require the introduction of alcohol-fueled engines, a requirement that focused the industry's product development energies on a technology that has found no market elsewhere in the world. During the period of 1982–1989, an average of 60 percent of the vehicles produced were alcohol-fueled. Meanwhile, the number of years each model was kept in production soared to 14 years in Brazil—almost four times the Japanese standards.

Although the Japanese lean production system was modernizing the world automotive industry, it did not hit Brazil until the early 1990s when the Brazilian government began opening its frontiers to import of whole vehicles and parts, introducing real competition to what was then a tight oligopoly. Such competition caught the Brazilian OEMs unprepared, exposing the industry's weaknesses to foreign competition and dramatically showing them how essential it was to reduce production costs while simultaneously providing better products.

Although the initial prices of imported vehicles were too high to attract a large mass of middle-class potential buyers, customers' perceptions and expectations were raised. Demand for lower-cost and more efficient cars also was increasing.

The first reaction of automakers to the threat of imports, even more aggra-vated by a stagnant domestic market, was to further develop the 1000-cc cars segment (Fig. 1).

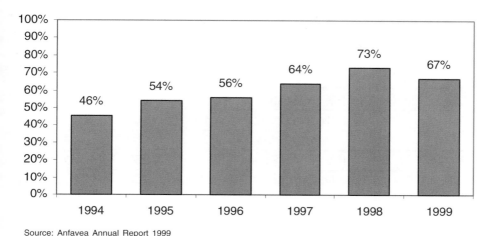

Source: Anfavea Annual Report 1999

Figure 1   Brazilian 1000-cc market share evolution (1984–1999).

Foreseeing some changes in the pattern of consumption, Fiat do Brasil began lobbying for a decrease of the tributary load on the 1000-cc vehicles. Other OEM companies took similar approaches, creating competition in prices and forcing movement toward modernization (cost competitiveness). However, this was a slow move. The investments toward modernization really began with the advent of globalization and economic stability introduced by the new currency, the real (R$).

The New Currency

The 1994 "Plano Real," a currency stabilization program, finally brought economic stability to the country. Impelled by the perspectives of a potential market of 3,000,000 vehicles/year (4,000,000 in Mercosul), the world industry settled en masse in the country, putting Brazil in the spotlight as today's country with the largest number of OEMs in the world (Fig. 2). Among others, the following companies have set up shop in Brazil: Toyota, Honda, DaimlerChrysler, Peugeot (PSA Group), Renault, Ásia Motors, and Audi. In addition to these OEMs, the already installed OEMs (Volkswagen, GM, Fiat, and Ford) have invested in modernization and new production units.

OEM	Vehicles	Investment (US$ Million)	Additional Capacity
Volkswagen/Audi	Golf, Audi A3, Light Truck	3,100	170
Fiat	Palio Pickup, Bravo, Croma	700	50
GM	Corsa, Blue Macaw, S10	4,180	150
Ford	KA, Fiesta, Ranger	2,250	100
Renault	Megane, Clio	750	120
DaimlerChrysler	A Class, Dakota	1,650	120
Ásia Motors	Topic Tower	700	70
Honda	Civic	340	80
Toyota	Corolla	100	100
PSA	106, 205, Citroën	1,000	100
Hyundai	H100/Accent	285	40
TOTAL		**15,055**	**1,140**

Source: Media and Companies

Figure 2   Investments of OEMs in Brazil (1996–2000).

Recently, in terms of investments, Brazil is second only to North America, according James Crate, editor of *Automotive News International.* Such investments are aimed at specific targets: increasing export capabilities, renewing quality standards, escaping from high taxes as well as from the regions influenced by labor unions, and developing new models of relationships with suppliers. These are described as follows:

- *Increase export capabilities*—The Brazilian car of the future is the one that can be exported to any country, not only to Argentina. Every OEM has invested in producing cars with global quality standards and the maximum quantity of parts supplied by the domestic industry. Many are very close or have already reached this goal. Five out of ten of last year's best-selling cars in the world were produced in Brazil, according to *Automotive World Magazine*—GM's Corsa and Astra, the Toyota Corolla, the Volkswagen Golf, and the Honda Civic.

- *Renewal of quality standards*—"The age of a construction does not reflects its productivity," says Volkswagen do Brasil President Demel. "But an old plant does not have to be a bad one," he adds. As noted, most of the 1960–1970 assembly plants installed in the country are outdated, facing serious internal logistics problems. For instance, Volkswagen is investing more than 1 billion U.S. dollars in modernizing its huge, 30-year-old plant in São Bernardo do Campo.

- *Escape from high taxes and regions influenced by strong labor unions*—Giving continuity to the industrial decentralization process currently underway in Brazil, OEMs are building new plants outside the traditional Southeast automotive industry center. Ford is installing its new plant in the Northeast. Six new plants are located in the southern state of Paraná, while two others are already planned. State taxes or other fiscal or legal incentives have been decisive on choosing new site locations.

- *Develop new relationship models with suppliers*—The four big OEMs have used Brazil as a testing laboratory for developing new relationship models with their suppliers, aiming for more lean production. These changes are empowering suppliers of complete assembled modules, or "systemists" as they are known. The systemists now operate on the same site as automotive manufacturers, delivering their components just-in-time directly to the vehicle assembly line. They are responsible for a large proportion of supply and have become powerful players in the procurement market, taking the production of smaller auto parts from the hands of the OEMs. Chrysler's Dakota pickup, for example, is built on a rolling chassis supplied by Dana, which manages 70 sub-suppliers. The new GM plant, where the Blue Macaw will be built, will start its operations with zero inventory. The suppliers will have 90 minutes to feed their components directly to the line. The Volkswagen plant located in Taubaté cut 11 million dollars in inventories in the last five years by using a just-in-time/Kanban logistics model.

This promising scenario, however, was struck by a series of unpredictable events. The year after reaching a new record of 2,067,000 vehicles produced in 1997, the world (and more seriously, some emerging markets such as Brazil) was hit by the Asian crisis. This and customers that were more demanding also held the market at lower levels—1,500,000 units produced in 1998.

The year 1999 was even worse, with 1,300,000 units produced. The decline was due to high interest rates and frightened consumers threatened by high unemployment rates. A declared moratoria from one of the Brazilian states was followed by a new exchange rate as a result of the currency devaluation implemented by the government. This fact negatively impacted the Mercosul agreement and fueled the deterioration of Argentina's economy—Brazil's largest export market. As stated by **GM do Brasil** President Frederick Hendersen, "1999 is over, and almost everything that could have gone wrong happened this year!"

In the 1990s, the Brazilian automotive industry tried to expand its domestic market through creative ways. However, now it is time to look for a sustained domestic market growth and, with a strong export plan, aim for the overseas market.

The New Millennium

As the new millennium begins, the economic scenario—with controlled inflation, growing GDP, and lower interest rates—seems more promising for Brazil. The production capacity is already installed and the quality of the products offered is world class.

Brazil's automotive industry has modernized its installations and expanded the capacity with newcomers. The established **OEMs** are developing new business strategies, new product lines, restructured management and production, and reformulated procurement. In addition, they have reduced the number of suppliers and introduced plant productivity incentives.

The basic changes and improvements needed to modernize the industry have been accomplished. Each OEM is now looking for different strategies to increase its competitive position. Fiat's Giovanni Razelli believes in aggressiveness. GM's Frederick Henderson is betting on a large product line. Volkswagen CEO Herbert Demel believes in quality, and Renault has opted for differentiation. However, they all share one common belief: optimism about the years to come.

Everyone agrees that the Brazilian market has immense untapped potential to grow, and investments by OEMs have given credibility to the market potential. Brazil and all South American markets continue to represent one of the regions with the higher potential of growth in the world because the "inhabitants per car" ratio is low, compared to that in the mature markets (Fig. 3).

Demand will not be satisfied until various daunting obstacles are overcome. The main hurdles are low purchasing power of the population, heavy taxation, high interest rates, and insufficient production scale. Unfortunately, most of these barriers are not under the control of the OEMs. A key question is: What else can be done to boost production in this new, highly competitive environment?

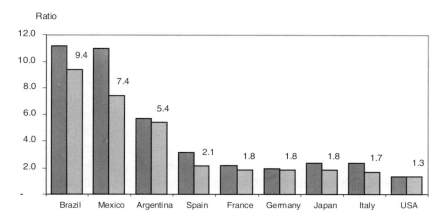

Source: Anfavea Annual Report 1999

Figure 3 Inhabitants per vehicle ratio (1988–1997).

At a time when the major concern of the industry is to achieve a higher economy of scale, companies face idle capacity. Automobile manufacturers must produce higher volumes to recapture increasing investments (Fig. 4).

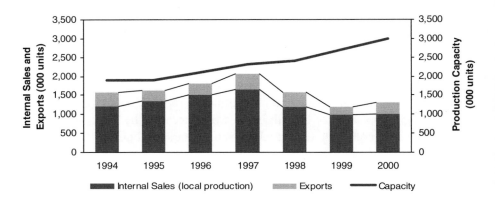

Source: Standard & Poor's DRI

Figure 4   Sales versus capacity (1994–2000).

Production capacity and competition have increased with the arrival of more than 15 new players in the last 5 years. Although these newcomers still have limited market power, the market leaders (Volkswagen and Fiat), which each holds 26 to 28 percent of the market share, are deemed to lose market share to the newcomers. None of the newcomers still offers a 1000-cc engine model (the so-called "popular cars"), and thus none is competing in the largest portion of the market. Renault will be the first to produce such a model—the new Clio 2—in the beginning of 2000. When other newcomers start following in Renault's steps, it will be hard for a leader to keep more than 15 percent of the market. "The popular cars will continue to dominate the Brazilian market," says GM's Henderson, and the tax advantages for such cars will always inhibit a better sales distribution among the different segments.

Complementing the reduction of taxes, the renewal of the national fleet is an efficient way to increase the domestic demand. The average age of the fleet is currently 10 years, and roughly 27 percent of the fleet is greater than 15 years old. Aiming for road safety, a cleaner environment, and an increase in demand, the National Transit Council (Contran) is forcing poorly maintained vehicles to be withdrawn from circulation. This could increase internal sales by 400,000 cars per year in a short period.

International interest rates and credit with longer financing periods are key variables that are within the jurisdiction of the government. The problem is that even if the government succeeds in keeping interest rates low and in maintaining a balanced internal budget, the domestic market will feel the effects only two to three years down the road.

Meanwhile, the best interim solution is to look for new market opportunities abroad. Last year's export figure was only 3.4 billion U.S. dollars, a 35 percent drop from the 1998 number of 5 billion U.S. dollars. The objective of Anfavea (the Brazilian Automakers Association) for the next few years is to climb back to the 5 billion U.S dollars level in exports. Potential market targets are Australia, China, India, Mexico, South Africa, and, obviously, the Mercosul.

Looking Beyond 2000

Both the government and the OEMs have their own homework to do. As the government battles for the establishment of structural reforms in the economy to create a basis for domestic market growth, the Brazilian automotive industry will continue to face dramatic changes over the next decade as markets grow, buying patterns change, and customers create new demands. The OEMs will require investments in areas such as brand management, e-commerce, new distribution channels, and customer service.

We believe that the stage is set for Brazil to continue its path to position itself as one of the leading players in the global automotive industry.

Challenges in the Global Truck Market—The Truck Industry on the Road to High Technology

Sylvia Enders

> *If you're going through hell, keep going.*
> —Winston Churchill

Introduction

In a world hyped by the information highway and the fact that in the virtual "e-conomy" distance no longer matters, some facts are here to stay—the transport of real goods will continue to be necessary. In a tangible world consisting of roads, new construction, and consumers demanding that goods be delivered, trucks globally provide the essential link between producer and customer. Furthermore, the importance of trucks in freight transportation will grow globally. In industrialized countries, train capacity is scarce, and intermodal transport models have shown that they do not to provide the necessary flexibility. In developing economies, the high investment in infrastructure is first directed into road networks.

Although the truck as a transport solution provider has remained essentially the same during the 100 years of its existence—revolutionary substitution products being hard to find—the global truck industry has undergone significant changes in the last decade. In constantly intensifying competitive pressure, a remarkable concentration process has taken place. In a market where production volumes are far below those we know from the car industry, size is crucial for manufacturers to achieve economies of scale. With the deregulation of the transport market, ever increasing pressure on profit margins of new truck sales

1 The author wishes to thank Mr. Wilhelm Walch for valuable discussions.

moved the business from a product to a service centered approach, including the marketing of used vehicles and the financial and fleet management services in the truck OEMs' value chain.

This chapter analyzes the present situation of the global truck industry and examines the emerging trends and challenges. Then it discusses the future key success factors and offers an outlook on how truck OEMs can be profitable in the future.

Analysis of the Global Truck Industry

Competitors

Concentration

Since the 1970s, the number of independent truck manufacturers has decreased significantly: in Europe, from more than 35 companies to fewer than 15 independent companies. The truck industry has become truly global, with a small number of powerful high-volume players and a strong presence in more than two world regions (Fig. 1). A network of global alliances, joint ventures, and cooperations offers access to many markets around the world. Consolidation presently has reached a very high level, but there is room for even more restructuring across regions.

The biggest player by far is DaimlerChrysler, which produced more than 240,000 units in 1998, more than twice as many trucks over 6 tons gross vehicle weight as the next biggest truck OEM, the American Navistar which produced 108,000 units (Fig. 2). They are followed by Volvo (84,400 units), whose recent attempt of a "Swedish merger" with Scania failed after restrictions by the EU. Both Navistar and the next biggest player, the American Paccar (84,000 units), so far have concentrated primarily on the North American market (the exception being Paccar's European DAF brand). The European players Renault Véhicules Industriels (with Mack in the United States), Iveco, and MAN all show a positive trend toward globalization, but they will definitely need to grow considerably to ensure their survival. GMC, one of the smaller U.S. players with a share in Isuzu (the biggest Japanese truck producer with 63,000 units) does not seem to follow a global integration strategy, whereas Scania (47,000 units), now part of the Volkswagen Group, is strongly globalized. The Japanese truck producers, such as Mitsubishi (Fuso) or Toyota (Hino), are relatively small

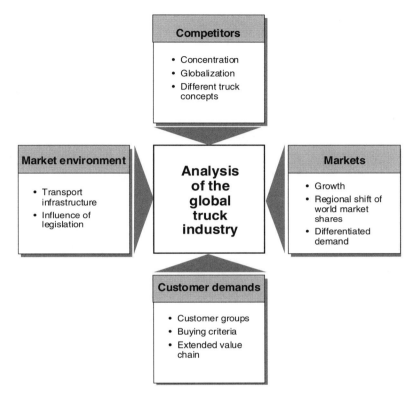

Figure 1   Analysis of the global truck industry.

(49,000 and 40,000 units in 1998, respectively) and show little globalization potential at the moment. They have mainly concentrated so far on medium heavy trucks and the Asia-Pacific region, but they seem to be planning for expansion of both their product range and their global presence.

Globalization

From a global perspective, the European truck OEMs have grown to control the biggest part of the world market, although regional dominance remains mostly in the hands of the home players (Fig. 2). Most major American truck makers (with the exception of Paccar, Navistar, and GMC) are now in European hands. The Europeans dominate emerging markets such as South America. The Asian truck markets are either in the hands of the Japanese

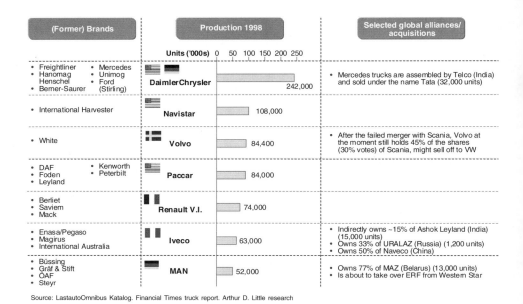

(Former) Brands	Production 1998	Selected global alliances/ acquisitions
	Units ('000s) 0 50 100 150 200 250	
• Freightliner • Mercedes • Hanomag • Unimog • Henschel • Ford • Berner-Saurer (Stirling) **DaimlerChrysler**	242,000	• Mercedes trucks are assembled by Telco (India) and sold under the name Tata (32,000 units)
• International Harvester **Navistar**	108,000	
• White **Volvo**	84,400	• After the failed merger with Scania, Volvo at the moment still holds 45% of the shares (30% votes) of Scania, might sell off to VW
• DAF • Kenworth • Foden • Peterbilt • Leyland **Paccar**	84,000	
• Berliet • Saviem • Mack **Renault V.I.**	74,000	
• Enasa/Pegaso • Magirus • International Australia **Iveco**	63,000	• Indirectly owns ~15% of Ashok Leyland (India) (15,000 units) • Owns 33% of URALAZ (Russia) (1,200 units) • Owns 50% of Naveco (China)
• Büssing • Gräf & Stift • ÖAF • Steyr **MAN**	52,000	• Owns 77% of MAZ (Belarus) (13,000 units) • Is about to take over ERF from Western Star

Source: LastautoOmnibus Katalog. Financial Times truck report. Arthur D. Little research

Figure 2   The world's major truck OEMs.

and Korean manufacturers (e.g., Malaysia, Thailand, or Indonesia) or remain virtually closed (China). The American truck OEMs to date have not secured significant global alliances. As the American market offers considerable volume, they could continue to thrive by focusing only on the local markets.

The current challenge that globalized OEMs are facing is to achieve bigger economies of scale by completely globalizing their product ranges. Companies strive to exploit global synergy potential throughout the value chain. As the "world truck" has so far remained a dream because customers' needs, preferences, and legislation are too different around the world, OEMs are streamlining their product programs by using global components.

Regionally Differing Truck Concepts

Until today, a considerable difference existed among the truck concepts of Japan, Europe, and North America. In America, customers favor component trucks, custom tailored to their needs with components of their choice. In fact, Freightliner, part of DaimlerChrysler since the mid-1980s, originated as a haulage company that started building its own machines because the existing trucks at that time simply did not fit their exact needs.

European manufacturers produce more integrated trucks, mainly using their own "identity components" (i.e., cab, powertrain, and axles). However, some components, such as gearbox, suspension, or brake systems, have been outsourced. The highest integration index traditionally can be found with Japanese OEMs.

The basic preferences for the different truck philosophies will prevail to a certain extent, but cost pressure and globalization have gradually brought the concepts closer together. Strong component suppliers such as Meritor or Eaton now supply major components to European OEMs. In the drive for global economies of scale, Europeans have started the implementation of their own components in their American trucks, whereas U.S. components, such as the Mack engine in Renault's heavy range, have found good acceptance in the European market. Another example of concept convergence is the Australian market, where trucks with a mixture of American and European features (e.g., RVI's Magnum Mack or Iveco's EuroStar and PowerStar) are highly successful.

Scania has already reached an outstanding level in the globalization of its product program. DaimlerChrysler, being big enough in most regions to sustain sufficient volumes, has so far followed a streamlining strategy mainly for production and sourcing processes, accepting regional product differences to a certain point. However, it is currently evaluating the additional globalization potential represented by interregional component exchange. Renault and Mack also have reached a reasonable globalization of their product ranges, the European Class 6 and 7 trucks having been in the U.S. market for more than a decade. However, considerable potential continues to exist (e.g., with axles).

Markets

The global truck market shows positive growth trends. In global competition, the major cards have been dealt. However, as developing markets, particularly Asia, grow stronger, the global positions of the different OEMs might shift somewhat in favor of the smaller Japanese OEMs. The considerable differences in the development stages of the markets make true globalization of the product ranges of OEMs difficult.

Growth

Global truck markets will show steady growth during the next years. The biggest truck market, the NAFTA region, and Western Europe will grow moderately, whereas the Asia-Pacific markets, particularly China and India, are predicted to grow by more than 10 percent per annum. Good growth potential can be expected from South America and Eastern Europe, whereas the African market remains insignificant. The NAFTA region will continue to account for the biggest global market share, but it considerably loses importance to China and the remainder of the Asia-Pacific region (Fig. 3). The growth perspectives differ considerably by segments. For instance, in Europe the medium and light segment shows very good growth perspectives because of a decline in package size and city transport policy enforcing weight restrictions for inner-city deliveries.

Regional Shift of World Market Share Offers Opportunities for Small Players

Given the right strategies, the global market positions of today could shift considerably. Companies that seem to be in a relatively weak position today regarding volume, such as Mitsubishi, Toyota, or MAN, could quickly improve their positions with the right cooperation and market strategies. In particular,

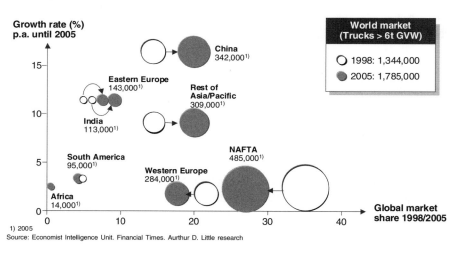

Figure 3 The global truck market today and tomorrow.

Japanese or Korean truck OEMs, which are small players measured on a global scale, are placed in a sound growth position with their strong presence in the promising Asian markets. Growth strategies based on alliances with Eastern European OEMs, such as MAN with MAZ (Belarus), also show potential. China, with an incredible market of 342,000 trucks (>6 tons GVW) in 2005, and India are most promising for the big European OEMs, which already have some alliances in those countries.

Differentiated Demand

In globally streamlining their product programs, OEMs also must differentiate their trucks according to market sophistication. Developing countries with poor-quality roads and low technical skills in workers still need robust and low-tech products. Industrialized markets are calling for high-tech trucks, with emphasis on specific transport solutions, usage optimization, and low-cost performance over the complete life cycle. This places even more restriction on product globalization.

Customers

Customer Groups

Customer demand in industrialized countries can be divided into on-road and off-road use, both calling for completely different specifications. Trucks designed for freight transportation today are sporting high-tech onboard electronic equipment (e.g., for communication), whereas trucks designed for off-road use (e.g., in the construction industry) will remain relatively "traditional." Because on-road use is by far the higher volume, and the changes in the business are quite fundamental, the next section of this chapter will concentrate on this segment, examining the industrialized markets.

The trucking firms can be divided into specialized transport providers and providers for the mass-transport market. The percentage of owner-operators has declined significantly. This concentration on the customer's side is mirrored on the manufacturer's side; that is, mass producers with high volume and homogeneous product range, versus highly specialized OEMs.

Trucking deregulation has led to increasing competition in the industry, initiating a worldwide trend to higher professionalism of truck operators. High rates of asset utilization are essential to the profitability of trucking companies, truck productivity being the operators' major concern. This applies not only to increased truck usage, but also to the retention of drivers—particularly in North America, where driver shortage has become a major concern.

Buying Criteria

Trucks are not pleasure or lifestyle products. Rather, their owners need them to conduct their businesses. Thus, buying decisions are based on an investment calculation focused on rational buying criteria:

- The solution of a specific transport problem
- The price
- The life-cycle cost of the trucks

Brand image also plays a role, because trust in the product is essential. In summary, fleet customers have extremely high expectations about the quality and performance of trucks to maximize uptime. They place increased emphasis on cost reduction for maintenance and a longer life cycle of components and systems.

Extended Value Chain

As customers have started to demand lifetime responsibility and service, and have begun to buy mileage instead of trucks, the value added created outside the gates of the OEMs has increased. The truck OEMs have shifted their sales strategies from a product/engineering focus to a service/life-cycle focus (Fig. 4). In the United States, where the trend for leasing trucks originated, huge leasing companies emerged. In Europe, OEMs extended their value chain and started their own leasing companies and used-truck centers to impede the intrusion of external competitors in capturing profit over the life cycle of the truck. Their strategic challenge has been to unite two completely different philosophies—a tangible product and an intangible service strategy— into one consistent portfolio. This strategy enables OEMs to serve varying customer needs with tailored bundles. It has also moved the business to a different battlefield and resulted in significant changes in the dealers' role and competence profile.

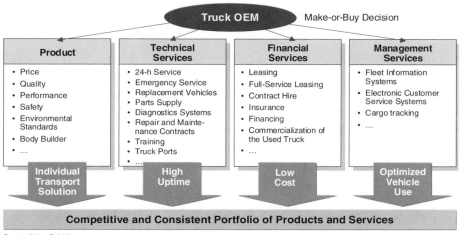

Source: Arthur D. Little

Figure 4   Truck OEMs' product and service portfolio.

Market Environment

Transport Infrastructure

In all industrialized countries, increasing congestion results in a detrimental effect on national economies. Therefore, considering freight transport growth projections, a solution to avoid the breakdown of the road transport system must be found quickly. Three solutions are possible to solve this dilemma: (1) more efficient use of trucks (leading to fewer trucks on the road), (2) more efficient use of the infrastructure by the introduction of intermodal systems, or (3) expansion of the infrastructure.

Intelligent transport systems for more efficient use of both the trucks and the existing infrastructure have already been developed. Computerized vehicle routing and scheduling systems and traffic guidance systems improve the efficiency of truck usage and have already shown significant cost-saving potential for truck operators. These systems are already widely used by large operators. Even if more advanced telecommunications technology brings further progress, much of the efficiency upgrading potential has already been realized. Thus, the congestion situation will not be much improved.

Intermodal transport systems require high investment, and to date they have not brought the expected benefits, primarily due to reduced flexibility and lack of railway capacity. The implementation of sophisticated automatic guidance and traffic control systems is technically possible, but that implementation is restricted by high investment in road infrastructure. Out of necessity, Japan, with its limited space, is probably most advanced in the implementation of such technology.

Because a significant expansion of the road network is unlikely in Europe, an increase in the productivity of long haulage trucks by raising the weight limit (currently 40 tons in most of Europe) seems to be a possible future solution. Similarly, the booming economy and worsening highway congestion in the United States may force the U.S. Congress to consider legislation to increase truck weight.

The Influence of Legislation

The truck industry is under high legislative pressure. Because of increasing public demands, governments are gradually imposing more restrictive emission standards. In Europe, legislation regarding gross vehicle and drive axle weights, as well as truck dimensions, is very different among the various countries. However, noise and exhaust emission standards are well harmonized. Unfortunately for the truck OEMs, the objectives of governments are ambitious and are not specified in a timely manner. This leads to high R&D costs. In the United States, the situation is similar, although the thresholds and testing methods are somewhat different from those in Europe.

Reducing emissions by improving engine technology has two barriers: time and cost. Time means that legislation must indicate as early as possible what the next emission standards will be to ensure that development can go in the right direction as early as possible. Cost means that faster innovation, if possible, is more expensive. Moreover, after a certain reduction, meeting the next threshold comes at a considerably higher price.

In general terms, more restrictive emission standards are to be expected globally, although it will take considerable time before the developing countries reach the level of industrialized countries. As all categories of engine technology are at hand in the programs of OEMs, a gradual advance will pose no problems for the industry and will be possible without additional R&D cost.

Trends in the Global Truck Industry

The competitive environment of the truck industry will remain marked by shakeouts. It will be "grow or go," especially for the medium-sized companies (40,000 to 60,000 units). This means that the OEMs cannot afford to relinquish global strategies, although they will have to find a sensible balance between concentration and reach, depending on their financial potential. The globally different growth perspectives and product requirements result in the need to develop differentiated world strategies: OEMs will focus on penetration/ market entry by cooperative ventures or acquisitions in new and developing markets. In the industrialized countries, a strategy of defending or improving market positions by increasing truck efficiency and expanding the service portfolio will be required.

Next to this challenge of further globalization to achieve the necessary size for survival, truck OEMs will face a continuously dynamic market situation with new developments in the area of product technology, distribution, and, on the customers' side, the transport environment (Fig. 5). In the future, the truck industry will be dominated by the use of high-tech applications such as electronics and modern information technology. As has happened in other industries, the Internet will be a significant driver of change for the existing business models which will, coupled with the competitive pressure of further globalization, create a highly challenging environment for truck OEMs.

Technology Trends

Modern truck technology is characterized by the increased use of electronics. It has two main drivers: better fulfillment of customer demands, and compliance with legislation.

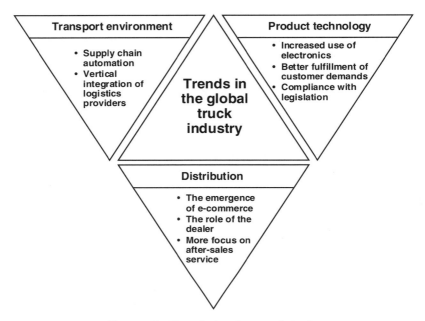

Figure 5   Trends in the truck industry.

Increased Use of Electronics

During the last decade, the formerly low-tech truck industry has gradually moved up the technology scale. However, not all high-tech features that are possible—for instance, applying methods or materials from the space or airplane industries—have actually been implemented. Cost pressure, government regulations, and the pragmatic approach of truck customers, who accept advanced technology only if it results in a positive effect on the profitability of the operation, will place some restraints on the use of high technology (Fig. 6). Nonetheless, many of the requirements of modern trucks will be fulfilled only by technologically advanced product features. The most important trend is that trucks, similar to cars, will rely more and more on the use of electronics. Not only are all major components electronically controlled; electronic functions will be integrated to permit the optimization of the performance of the entire system (e.g., the complete powertrain).

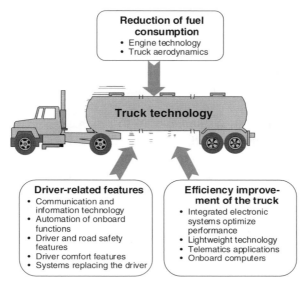

Figure 6   Product technology trends to improve the fulfillment of customer demands.

Better Fulfillment of Customer Demands

Reduction of Fuel Consumption

Reducing fuel consumption has already come a long way, mainly because of the use of electronic fuel injection systems. The possibility of further enhancing fuel economy by improved engine technology requires extremely high R&D cost and long development times. That is why improvement of fuel efficiency is no longer focused only on engine technology, but also on the aerodynamics of the truck. An improvement of the drag coefficient of heavy trucks to passenger car levels promises outstanding positive fuel consumption effects. This was demonstrated by Scania's model of a concept truck that was presented in Brussels during the end of 1999. Now a prototype of the truck is already running on Scania's trial grounds in Södertälje.

Efficiency Improvements of the Truck

Efficiency improvements can be achieved related to truck performance (e.g., durability or loading capacity) as well as usage. Multiple efforts have been made in both directions. Integrated systems with electronic control optimize driveline performance and reduce wear and tear. Electronic brake technology optimizes average speed while making no concession to security. Built-in devices for maintenance monitoring facilitate service according to requirements, instead of having to follow predetermined intervals. This will result in considerable cost savings potential for operators.

Lightweight technology is another way to achieve better truck efficiency. DaimlerChrysler currently is testing a concept truck featuring an aluminum chassis construction, saving up to 700 kg in weight for a long-haulage trailer. The use of new materials for cabin construction that Daimler has tried with Unimog (use of carbon-fiber composite material used in airplane construction) is not likely to be widely adopted because high production costs outweigh the multiple advantages such as weight savings or corrosion resistance.

Telematics applications in trucks help to improve efficient usage of the vehicle. This comprises, for instance, the increasing use of sophisticated communications technology and navigation systems in the truck. Navigation packages enable operators to determine the precise location of the truck and to communicate truck location information to dispatch. Logistics manager programs coordinate tracking, dispatch, and remote diagnostics.

Onboard computers, such as Freightliner's Truck Productivity Computer, serve as a gateway to information about the status of the vehicle, as well as vehicle operation. A driver performance monitor tracks information related to fuel economy, trip miles, leg miles, and driver work hours (electronic log book). This type of fleet management system will give fleet operators additional information for evaluating drivers' performance and can support replacement decisions as the vehicle history is recorded automatically.

Safety, Comfort, and Work Environment of Truck Drivers

The enhanced use of communication and information technology will lead to new profiles and roles for drivers, creating much higher expectations for driver competencies. Systems reducing the driver workload in handling the truck by automated or semi-automated onboard functions will be implemented. Meritor and ZF in a joint venture recently developed an automated mechanical transmission called FreedomLine, which completely eliminates manual clutch actuation. This facilitates the performance of other tasks. This is a benefit to the driver who needs to increasingly act as a high-level communication interface between dispatch and cargo, as well as the client. For instance, the driver must perform more and more of the dispatcher's tasks.

Although facilitating truck driving (and thus taking away the macho image of truck drivers) has encountered some driver resistance, drivers adapt astonishingly well to the new circumstances and technology. As it happens, truck drivers have become one of the fastest-growing groups of Internet users in the United States.

To increase truck and highway safety, "driver friendly" interfaces with easy-to-use controls or easy-to-read displays are installed to prevent distracting the vehicle operator from the driving task. Innovative systems such as Freightliner's Lane Guidance System warn the driver in case he accidentally drifts off the lane.

Driver comfort features, such as sleeper accommodations or washing and cooking facilities, will become increasingly important for the North American market because driver retention is a key issue for truck operators. On the other hand, the trend in Europe is going toward high-tech interchangeable units with elevated efficiency but without special driver comfort.

There is even a vision of the implementation of completely automated systems or remote control, so that drivers would no longer be necessary, especially in urban areas, cargo ports, or on special truck lanes. Parts of this vision are already technologically feasible. DaimlerChrysler's Promote Chauffeur "electronic towbar" uses permanent wireless communication controlling the hydraulic steering, and the electronic brake and transmission systems, and a video/infrared monitoring system enables the combined steering of several trucks without mechanical connection.

Compliance with Legislation Regarding Emissions

Increasingly restrictive emission standards are placing constant pressure on the innovation capabilities of OEMs. Fuel cells, one innovation to note, may provide a zero emission alternative. The fuel cell is already available, but its efficiency must increase considerably before it can be applied in long-haul traffic.

In an effort to find solutions for a cleaner environment, several U.S. government agencies and the truck industry have teamed together in an initiative called "21st Century Truck" led by the U.S. Army. For this program, Volvo, Lockheed Martin Control Systems, and Radian have built a demonstrator Class 8 tractor powered by a hybrid electric propulsion system. Vehicles featuring this kind of alternative engine technology probably will find their first broad acceptance in urban-area buses.

Noise is largely influenced by tires. Future tire technology offers vast improvement potential regarding noise emission and, as an additional positive effect, improved durability, traction, and security.

Trends in Distribution

The Emergence of e-Commerce

As the focus of the sales strategy has shifted from product to service, the distribution function and the dealer profile have been redefined. With the Internet acting as an enabler, distribution and the role of the independent dealer will change fundamentally again. The emergence of e-commerce more and more questions the sales function of dealers. This development is enhanced by the increasing importance of direct sales by OEMs as fleet sizes grow. In the future, dealers may no longer be involved in pricing because this could be negotiated directly between the manufacturer and the customer.

So far, the possibilities of truck sales via the Internet are restricted by the complexity of the product and the user-specific needs. As truck OEMs and component suppliers move toward a more modular approach to building a vehicle, integrating powertrain components and onboard electronics, trucks become more susceptible to being sold by e-commerce. This would mean a further reduction of the already small margins in new truck sales.

The Role of the Dealer

In spite of these developments, distribution will not cease to exist, and the value of human contact and personal attention must not be underestimated. However, dealers will prosper in the new world order only if they provide intimate customer and market knowledge. They will depend fully on exact and comprehensive customer analysis. (How can I retain customers in a long-term relationship and keep them in my dealership over the complete life cycle of the truck? Which customer is profitable?) Only dealerships with excellent management and efficiency in all relevant processes will survive in this demanding environment.

There are many ways by which information technology helps dealers improve efficiency. For example, the ordering process will be further revolutionized by new applications of EDI, communication technology will optimize the organization of service, and virtual warehouses will lead to the optimization of dealers' parts supply.

The effective use of information technology will be crucial for the dealer to succeed. The availability of exact information at exactly the place and time needed will be the basis for specialized consultancy and problem solving, as well as in the resulting customer satisfaction. This applies to the knowledge of the salesperson, as well as to more efficient and higher-quality service and support. Information is freely available via the Internet, so customers are much better informed and increasingly buy benefits, not products. The role and competence profile of sales personnel must be redefined. They will have to apply a problem-solving approach and develop ways to create profit for customers by consultation selling.

The training needs of sales and service personnel are becoming more intense as the level of qualification required rises. This relates to product knowledge, which can be efficiently enhanced by computer-based training modules, but even more to behavioral training to enable sales and service personnel to perform in the changing environment. This investment by the dealer will offer payback only if personnel turnover rates are low. The emphasis will be more on excellent human resource management (e.g., the implementation of per-formance-oriented, motivating payment schemes throughout the team involved in the value creation process). The same type of payment method must be implemented in supporting functions also because overall efficiency is crucial.

More Focus on After-Sales Service

A decline in new truck sales margins, ultimately maybe even the loss of the sales function, forces the dealer to focus on after-sales service. Even in this previously profitable area, dealers are in an increasingly difficult position because products are becoming more sophisticated. This leads to higher investment in service technology, at a time when reduced service needs translate into lower usage of service equipment and longer intervals between the times when customers come to the workshop.

The dealers' position further erodes as trucks evolve to the point where service records are stored onboard and diagnosis information is readily available to anyone having the tools to extract it electronically.

Taking service one step further, truck makers are preparing to sell guaranteed vehicle uptime. This "sealed hood" approach would directly affect truck operator profits by providing an exact cost calculation basis and could further prohibit the entrance of external competitors into the service business.

Trends in the Transport Environment

Supply Chain Automation (SCA) as the Next Challenge After "Just-in-Time"

Truck operators as transport service providers are part of a complex system that is currently undergoing significant changes. Again, the Internet is revolutionizing the business landscape as business transactions (e.g., between manufacturers and suppliers) are brought online. Connectivity is extended to every element of the supply chain, including trucks.

In modern supply chain management, improving the complex interactions among organizations, materials, locations, and people is a vital necessity. First came the business process re-engineering initiatives of the last decades, which resulted in lean production concepts. Next was the consequence for the transport industry of the challenge of just-in-time delivery. Now companies are climbing the next step: supply chain automation with the help of sophisticated software applications. Implementation requires a first phase in which the supply chain of individual companies is optimized and automated. In the second phase, the supply chain of different interdependent companies is included. The Internet acts as an enabler for easy global intra- and intercompany communication. Parallel to company initiatives, supply chain automation technology is evolving rapidly, leading to additional functionalities of SCA. For trucking firms, that means the necessity of even more flexible delivery. It goes without saying that the trucking company—and each individual truck— will be part of the communication network.

Vertical Integration of Logistics Providers

In the context of more integrated transport systems, the availability of a variety of logistics services increasingly becomes a success factor. Logistics providers who own the entire transport data stream will be the leaders. Product and service portfolios from different industries are brought together to improve the market position of the supply-chain service providers. An interesting example is Ryder integrating its i2s Rhythm and Ryderlink software, thus providing an overview and controlling tool for supply-chain integration—in addition to offering the trucks for the actual transport, shipment tracking and tracing, and other related services. SAP has a similar agreement with Federal Express.

Key Success Factors for Meeting the Challenges of the Future

The challenges that a truck OEM will face in the future relate to all elements of the value chain (Fig. 7). In procurement, new models of working with suppliers must be found. The increased use of new technologies, coupled with the necessity to constantly assess customer willingness to accept higher cost, confronts design and development with a new challenge on the implementation of innovation, as we have seen previously in this chapter. To achieve low-cost production, they must follow up on the efforts of the past and further globalize their product programs to realize more economies of scale. In distribution, new partners (that is, the dealers as contributors to the success of the last stage of value creation) must be integrated into the product creation process.

Procurement and Low-Cost Production

Globalization has already led to the consolidation of the supply base. As the trend continues to use modular systems and to realize the still considerable cost-saving potential of globalizing components, the choice of suppliers and the mode of cooperation with them presents a major challenge to truck OEMs. Strong players in the supplier industry have interesting opportunities in this area.

Buying Criteria	Value Chain			
	Procurement	Design and Development	Production	Marketing, Sales, and After Sales
Providing a transport solution		• Technical specifications • Modular systems		• Consultancy about adequate specification • Connection to body builders
Price	• Contracts with suppliers	• Design and development for easy assembly	• Low cost	• Efficient distribution function • Financial services
Life cycle cost		• Design and development for • durability • low fuel consumption • easy maintenance	• Quality	• Service packages • Cost of spare parts • Cost of service hours
Uptime	• Supply with spare parts	• Design and development for • reliability • easy maintenance	• Quality	• 24-h service • Quality of service
Image	• Suppliers' brands	• Advanced technology	• Quality	• Marketing (brand) • Efficient, competent, friendly dealers

"All In One approach Package

Source: Arthur D. Little

Figure 7   Truck OEMs' key success factors along the value chain.

Systems integration, particularly the electronic architecture, is crucial to the overall performance and manageability of the truck and thus will become fundamental in the search for competitive advantages. This raises major questions for the future concerning the development of supplier market dynamics. Will there be systems suppliers, such as in the car industry? How will the OEMs manage to keep their integration role? Certainly, the way that American OEMs have worked with their component suppliers can serve as an example, but the integration of electronic architecture represents a much more sophisticated challenge than classic component integration.

Even if OEMs in general tend to outsource more complex systems, truck OEMs will still want to have the integrating competence and thereby govern the process. However, the role of suppliers could be redefined. Alliances, cooperations, joint ventures, and the implementation of revolutionary production concepts such as Volkswagen's Resende plant in Brazil might prove interesting alternatives to follow in the quest for the ideal integration index.

Distribution

Truck OEMs must reconsider marketing and sales. In a cost-centered approach, they need to implement an efficient method of distribution, including all opportunities connected with e-commerce. At the same time, they must offer effective solutions to their customers related to providing advice during purchase and providing a first-class after-sales service.

For truck OEMs, managing modern distribution potentially will include the implementation of OEM-owned dealerships, as well as the partnering with independent dealers. OEMs will have to handle an entire network of suppliers of competencies and service. They will more and more have to realize the importance of the parts and service business as new truck margins continue to shrink.

Thus, sophisticated network management will be essential for their future success. OEMs will need to include the dealers' perspective as an extension of the value chain and support strong partners by including them in their information network.

The Management of Innovation as the Governing Key Success Factor

After the big step from product focus to service focus, truck OEMs will have to manage the integration of their business into the "e-conomy" as the next leap forward. Overlaying all the previously mentioned key success factors will be the fact that throughout the entire value chain, the management of innovation will be crucial to the OEM (Fig. 8). Suggestions for implementation of innovation strategies can be found in subsequent chapters of this book.

Conclusion

Future success in the truck industry will depend on the ability of manufacturers to produce technologically advanced, high-quality, productive commercial vehicles and to provide superior services to truck operators, who expect solutions that help them to succeed in an increasingly competitive environment. As the trucking industry becomes more and more high tech, a new market

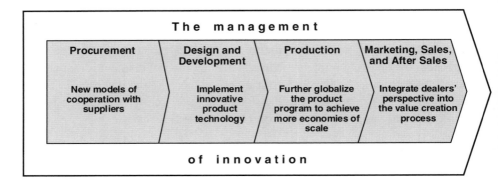

Figure 8   The management of innovation as the governing key success factor.

space is defined, and the competitive landscape will continue to change fundamentally. The foundations for an accelerated deployment of new technology must be laid now.

The next milestones in the truck industry can be expected soon. Because it is "grow or go" for several OEMs, we certainly will see more concentration of the industry. The likely candidates for mergers or acquisitions are RVI, Iveco, Navistar, and Hino. With the spectacular growth perspectives of some emerging markets, we will have to watch Asia, particularly China and India. Whoever finds a good strategy to enter these markets (e.g., by cooperative ventures or takeovers) will be in an excellent position for the future. Brazil, with its big market for Class 8 trucks, might continue to tempt American truck OEMs to move into that country.

As the telecommunications and electronics industries drive all other industries, we might see comparable effects on the truck industry. New players, particularly in the supplier industry, will gain importance, and new customer needs, such as "connectivity anytime, anywhere" will influence product features. This development has already started on the distribution side, as the Ryder example has shown. Another distribution milestone might be seen in a further split of the sales and service function. The challenge to OEMs to find the right strategy regarding OEM-owned versus independent dealers will offer another interesting area to watch.

Good opportunities exist in the truck industry. The coming years will show which manufacturers will master this transition on the road to high technology. In a few years, we certainly will see the number of independent truck OEMs decline again.

Literature

CFS Task Force "Electronic Commerce," Evolution—How Electronic Commerce Is About to Change Your Relationship with Your Truck OEM, Internet site www.cfshq.com, 1999.

Diez, Willi, "Trends in the International Truck Business." Presented at the VII Fenabrave Congress, São Paulo, Brazil, 1997.

Enders, Sylvia, Die künftige Rolle des Vertragshandels im Nutzfahrzeugvertrieb, in: Internationaler Nutzfahrzeugvertrieb im Wandel, Fachveranstaltung anläßlich der Nutzfahrzeug-IAA 1998 in Hannover, VDA/Institut für Automobilwirtschaft, Geislingen, 1998.

EurotransportMediaVerlags- und Veranstaltungs GmbH, Lastauto Omnibus Katalog 2000, Stuttgart, 1999.

Gapp, Dr.-Ing. Klaus-Peter, "Wachstumsmarkt Supply Chain Automatisierung," in *Information Management & Consulting*, Vol. 14 , No. 4, 1999, pp. 87–91.

Jonash, Ronald S., and Sommerlatte, Tom, *The Innovation Premium, How Next Generation Companies Are Achieving Peak Performance and Profitability*, Perseus Books, Reading, MA, 1999.

Karsten, Dr. Holger, and Achenbach, Jan, "Weltnetze besser steuern," in *Automobilproduktion*, 10/99, 1999, pp. 138–140.

Kennett, Pat, "Trucking into the 21st Century," *Financial Times Management Report*, London, 1998.

Kern, Michael, Visionen: Lkw im 21. Jahrhundert, lastauto omnibus 1/2000, Stuttgart, 2000, pp. 22–28.

McKay, Stuart, "The Truck Dealer Environment of the Future," presented at the Truck Dealer Forum at the IOMTR World Congress 1998, Wellington.

Svantesson, Lennart, *Developments and Global Trends in the Truck Industry*, Arthur D. Little, Stockholm, 1998.

Integration of Global R&D Operations at General Motors

Thomas E. Anderson

Introduction

Becoming a truly global company entails more than becoming global in product offerings and sales, even more than becoming global in manufacturing and engineering. The global company requires a global R&D activity as well, both to resource technologies effectively and to respond to diverse customer needs in varied global markets. In the case of technology acquisition, as the worldwide technical base continues to develop and expand, it becomes increasingly necessary to establish a local presence at a number of locations to access new knowledge and research results from foreign universities, institutes, and competitors.

At the same time, worldwide competitive pressures in the automotive industry dictate that automotive firms must move new products from development to market at an increasing pace, and satisfy local differences in market demand while implementing best practice engineering and manufacturing. This trend is not unique to the automotive industry, and technologically driven industries from pharmaceuticals to electronics are establishing global R&D networks. (W. Kuemmerle, *Harvard Business Review*, March 1997, pp. 61–70)

The driving forces toward globalization of R&D include: linking more closely to customers and markets globally, rapid deployment of product and process technologies throughout the business, and access to technology globally (Fig. 1). Although cost of R&D is sometimes mentioned as a driver, in fact, in the short term the added costs of coordination negate many of the salary and overhead cost benefits of locating in a lower-cost environment. Over the long term, as emerging market economies develop to support a healthy marketplace, the cost differential for R&D also tends to erode and can be supported only through productivity gains. Thus, access to customers, access to technology, and opportunities for rapid and full deployment truly represent the most valid rationale for globalization of R&D activities.

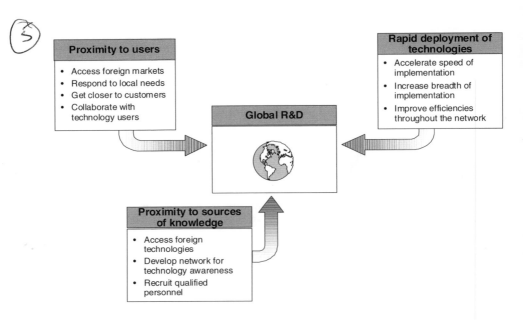

Figure 1   Driving forces for globalization of R&D.

The successful R&D organizational networks are based on an understanding of the dynamics of global R&D and a strong linkage between corporate strategy and R&D strategy. It is the integration of geographically distinct locations and distributed resources of people and facilities that allows the network to function in a coordinated manner.

General Motors Global R&D

Recently, General Motors integrated its research and development activities around the world under the functional umbrella of General Motors Global R&D Operations. The corporate alignment of worldwide R&D activities is a natural outgrowth of the company's expansion of global business operations.

A global R&D function allows the company to set corporate-wide strategic R&D directions consistent with a defined technology strategy, and to leverage its global technical resources to speed innovation into GM's global product offerings. This chapter describes the factors that led to this decision and gives a "work-in-progress" report on the implementation of a functionally integrated global R&D network.

Historically, the General Motors Research Laboratories served as a centralized corporate research activity for General Motors, but with a strong focus toward issues important to the North American marketplace. As GM's global business continued to expand and as growth opportunities more frequently were recognized to be in global markets, the need to expand the vision and reach of GM's internal R&D became apparent. The first step was the addition of specific research projects within the R&D portfolio to address global technology needs. In some cases, these technologies were relatively unimportant to the North American market but represented a significant opportunity when the global market was considered. In addition, the need to pursue R&D opportunities on a globally integrated scale is consistent with globalization of technology sourcing for products and manufacturing processes, and recognizes the growing impossibility of internally creating all innovation required for corporate competitiveness.

The globalization of commerce has necessitated the increased spread of technology dispersion and heightened awareness to the technological capabilities of suppliers, universities, and laboratories throughout the world. Through a globally integrated R&D organization, with local contacts to centers of expertise outside General Motors, it becomes feasible to maintain an awareness of, and interaction with, leading-edge technologies throughout the world. Conversely, the same integrated network facilitates implementation and dissemination of technology throughout the General Motors organization, thus greatly enhancing the benefit of innovation.

Effective globalization of the R&D organization requires an alignment of strategy, processes, organization, and resources, as outlined in Fig. 2. This familiar graphical representation shows the interrelationship of each of these areas, supported by continuous organizational learning and improvement. Starting with a set of strategic objectives for globalization, necessary processes to support those objectives are defined, required organizational changes (if any)

are assessed, and necessary interfaces are established to manage resources and coordinate activities. As will be seen in the following discussion, this functional restructuring creates a virtual organization rather than an administrative realignment to facilitate coordination and to minimize administrative and coordination costs.

Strategy
- What are our strategic objectives in becoming global?
  - Access to international resources and expertise
  - Improved technical intelligence globally
  - Closer relations with all GM customers
  - Improved efficiency and productivity
- Where in the world should we focus our attention?
- How should we expand globally?

Processes
- What new/significantly changed processes will be required to operate globally?
- How to minimize coordination costs while achieving functional coordination?
- Proper balance of local and global processes? Which tasks should be performed concentrated and which distributed?
- How to maintain effective links to all business unit customers and balance divergent needs?

Resources
- How to identify and coordinate resources around the world?
- Information system issues and compatibility?
- Where are unique technical skills available and at what cost?

Continuous Learning
- How do we ensure that competencies are enhanced on a continuous basis?
- How do we ensure that knowledge and technology are transferred between sites effectively?

Organization
- What is the appropriate organization structure? How centralized or decentralized?
- How do we align all locations around the world and agree on priorities for limited resources?
- How do we operate globally while meeting local requirements?

Figure 2   Globalization requires alignment of strategy, processes, organization, and resources.

Functional Global Organization

In the case of GM, the initial step toward a globally integrated R&D operation has been the establishment of the Technology Strategy Board, a council of senior executives whose charter is to align the corporation's long-term strategic technology direction with business plans of the operating units. This council is responsible to GM's Corporate Strategy Boards and ultimately to the Board of Directors for establishing and continuing to review GM's technology strategy and the elements needed for competitive success.

Global R&D Coordination

The leaders of R&D functions at 14 GM business units around the world are responsible for aligning GM global R&D resources and establishing global R&D competency networks in response to the corporate technology strategy. More specifically, the mandate is to:

- Develop and coordinate global competency networks in core business areas

- Resource global teams for major focused R&D programs

- Coordinate the global R&D project portfolio

- Provide a basis for a worldwide awareness of technology advances

This forum allows key R&D leaders around the world to become more aware of advances wherever they might occur and to identify opportunities within General Motors to capitalize on new technology and business opportunities.

Thus, GM has established a virtual organization composed of centers of R&D activities worldwide that provides coordination without changing administrative reporting relationships. This functional alignment and common agreement on technology strategy and project priorities will enable GM to better manage its global resources. The combination of technology needs, market focus, and regional autonomy with coordination has resulted in a network of coordinated R&D centers with strong centers of excellence that are technology focused. This structure, shown in the top center of Fig. 3, will support agility and speed as well as coordination of resources and focus on the highest-priority technology opportunities.

Role of Suppliers

12.

Suppliers also play a critical role in the global R&D network of GM. There is increased emphasis on collaboration at all levels. Rather than simply expecting suppliers to bid on specifications, new technologies from suppliers are evaluated for application in GM products and processes. In addition, technology can flow in the other direction as well, with suppliers playing a role as business partners in

Key area: demonstrate ATCD's
@ USCAR to reduce investment burden of supplier

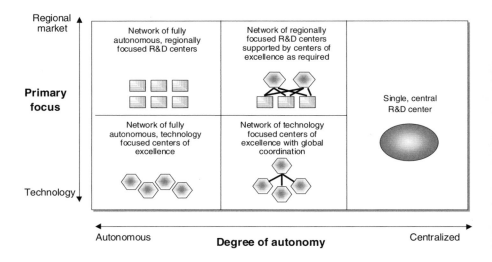

Figure 3   Functional organization is dependent on focus and strategy.

deploying GM-originated technology, especially those that fall outside the core business of General Motors. Finally, suppliers may serve as co-developers of certain technologies, enabling a quicker route from research and invention to commercialization. In short, although the specific role for suppliers will depend on the specifics of both the technology and the business issues, suppliers clearly can be key players on technology innovation teams.

In this new relationship, General Motors will not be on only the receiving end of the technology supply chain. Co-development is a two-way street. New technology invented at GM that is not directly related to core businesses is being made available to qualified, interested suppliers. In essence, the doors of GM research are being opened to supplier partners. This will greatly expand the commercialization capabilities available to GM and will speed availability of new technology for product.

Current Initiatives

As part of this new approach to R&D, GM's Worldwide Purchasing and Technology Planning groups have been working with R&D to set up innovation teams that link global implementation platforms with GM researchers, as well as with scientists and engineers at suppliers' R&D centers. These innovation teams provide a mechanism for fast technology development by combining the capabilities and minds of the supplier community, the R&D organization, and the targeted operating customer, all working together with clear technology targets and accelerated development and delivery schedules.

Further, technology interchange forums for suppliers have been initiated to expose the best technology of suppliers to the GM engineering and research community and to allow GM to present major technology challenges. These major challenges are handled somewhat through skunk-works projects, except the assignments are more broadly defined. The assignments are focused on addressing a need, similar to the challenge brought by John F. Kennedy to Congress in the 1960s, when he asked, "Can we land a man on the moon by the end of the decade?" GM is asking similar far-reaching questions: Can the tradeoff between crashworthiness and weight be eliminated in designing vehicles? How do we balance demand for increasingly intelligent vehicles with drivers' desire for full control of the car? Can we build and market a practical and affordable fuel cell vehicle by 2004?

These questions do not have easy answers, but attempting to address them can lead to "game changing" technologies—breakthroughs that cannot be easily matched by the competition. A single mission challenge, such as one of these, is a way to focus and organize technology development. It also imposes a systems perspective, which helps identify and draw in technology partners in the early stages.

GM has already begun to establish joint innovation teams involving suppliers. The GM R&D organization partnered with a supplier the GM Truck Group to develop and commercialize a new type of radiator fan clutch that incorporates a unique magneto-rheological fluid technology to modulate its operation. This technology promises a significant improvement in fuel economy over conventional hydraulic systems and will be an industry first, worldwide.

GM also worked with global suppliers to develop GMBond, an entirely new, environmentally friendly sand binder for casting of aluminum. This GM-invented technology has been recognized as a breakthrough by the American Foundrymen's Society, which called it "the development with the greatest long-term significance for the cast metals industry." The GMBond material is inexpensive, easy to use, recyclable, and non-toxic. The demonstration of production-rate usability is the final step toward commercialization and wide-spread availability.

From a global perspective, a need exists for direct-injection engines that are capable of tolerating North American fuels with high sulfur and clean diesel DI engines. This will require research-to-research collaboration with suppliers, as well as research-to-development collaboration because, given the significant challenges facing the world today, cooperation on technology is a business imperative. As we saw in Kyoto, the challenge of "clean and green" is very real and global in scope. Global warming is clearly a global issue, and coordinated R&D will enable GM to access and apply the best technology globally to address this challenge. Clearly, the developed nations must make a substantial improvement from where they are today. However, the developing countries also must use the best technologies the world has to offer so that, as their economies grow and flourish, we continue our forward momentum toward "clean and green" values. This means we must adopt new technology paradigms.

A strategy for advanced powertrain development is of critical importance to address growing environmental, energy, and societal issues. As the world population continues to expand rapidly, pressure increases on the environment and the earth's precious natural resources. General Motors has a host of advanced automotive technologies that can help achieve "clean and green" goals. Also, as a global company, GM can introduce these technologies to the appropriate markets.

The appropriate technologies range from alternative-propulsion hybrid vehicles (that have the potential to halve carbon dioxide emissions, achieve near-zero exhaust emissions, and provide two to three times the energy efficiency of current products) to the electric vehicle technology introduced by GM, which remains one of the best solutions for reducing noise and pollution in the large city centers of the world. Unfortunately, there is no clear choice on what future requirements will be and which technologies will best address them. Therefore, GM is focusing on a few critical options for leadership in energy efficiency and environmental quality.

GM Powertrain's recent realignment of operations directly supports this initiative with an immediate goal of improving the powertrain design and development cycle time. In addition, global focus project teams are in place for direct-injection engines, continuously variable transmissions, and automatic manual transmissions. The distribution and coordination of these activities allows the coordination of unique capabilities found at each partner globally, while avoiding duplication of effort and resources.

Summary and Conclusions

This chapter describes work in progress. The transformation from a centralized research laboratory, loosely coupled to engineering development centers around the world, to a coordinated global R&D organization is a large undertaking. The approach GM has undertaken should allow balance of the (sometimes) divergent expectations of business unit customers (Fig. 4) because the linked network can address both local and corporate needs. Fast innovation and execution is the name of the game. GM's new Global R&D Operations is structured to move quickly and flexibly on a wide range of technology options—by building the power of GM's collective resources through implementation of a global management process that fosters clear customer focus, sound strategy, and flawless execution.

Think Long Term	Deliver Results Today
Grow	Perform
Achieve Global Scale	Be Locally Responsive
Extend Functional Depth	Extend Cross Functionality
Innovate	Be Efficient
Become Flexible	Standardize

Figure 4   Expectations of R&D organization are varied.

A strategic vision has been developed, and the first global focus programs have been initiated. Programs are continually being defined in response to both market pressures and scientific discoveries, and these will be prioritized in relation to ongoing programs and appropriately resourced. Through coordination of resources, people, and facilities, the capability of GM's Global R&D Operations will be fully utilized and accelerate the pace of industry-leading innovations that are customer-driven, strategically focused, and lead to a sustainable competitive advantage for GM.

Literature

Kuemmerle, W., *Harvard Business Review*, March 1997, Boston, MA, pp. 61–70.

Factors Determining Success in the Product Creation Process in the 21ˢᵗ Century: Innovation and Engineering Execution

Andreas Feige, Robert Crooker

> *An idea that is not dangerous*
> *does not deserve to be called an idea.*
> —Oscar Wilde

The battle for future world market share soon will start to be fought on two fronts: at the interface to the customer and in the area of product creation. Competitive advantages will go to manufacturers that exploit innovation and engineering in the process of product creation.

Innovation generally is associated to some extent perhaps with rather absent-minded researchers or the "think tanks" of major companies. Thus, at first glance, it may seem hard to reconcile innovation with engineering execution, which deals with development jobs in a process similar to that of manufacturing. The following chapter discusses what is meant by the terms "innovation" and "engineering execution," the main factors that determine their success, and how they fit into the process of product creation.

Significance of the Product Creation Process

Critics may question whether this high level of importance really can be attributed to the product creation process and whether perhaps the successful subcontracting of development and production work to companies such as Bertone, Pininfarina, or Karmann actually proves that competence in this field is readily replaceable. The authors partly agree with this assertion. It is not necessary for all links in the value-creating chain to be produced in-house for all vehicle segments. Even important areas can be outsourced. However, the manufacturer must know what his core competency is and not outsource this as well. The ability to focus on core competencies in the product creation process represents a prerequisite for meeting the challenges within the future competitive landscape.

The motor industry is facing a grueling test, driven by globalization and over-capacity. This has resulted in a downward spiral in price and has created a shift in the status of the motor vehicle, robbing it of its position as a status symbol and turning it into one more example of ordinary consumer goods ("the car as a commodity"). At the same time, consumers are demanding more and more. This results in a tough price competition and a battle for market share combined with a continued consolidation of key players among OEMs and component manufacturers. The only manufacturers to survive will be those with the lowest costs, the best vehicle concepts, and the best consumer data and relationships. This shows clearly that a key factor in ensuring survival is the product creation process.

The Challenge

The challenge in the product creation process lies in developing a vehicle concept that is as fascinating as possible while meeting future customer requirements. The best concepts also are the ones that can be executed ("engineering execution") in the shortest possible time with the lowest pos-sible product costs and the highest possible quality.

The significance of product costs is still frequently underestimated. However, if one considers that the existing overcapacity is roughly equivalent to the total number of vehicles being sold today in South America and Western Europe, or, in other words, approximately 18 million units, one can see the potential threat very clearly. With an inevitability that can almost be measured, price battles will usher in a downward spiral (Fig. 1), at the end of which only those OEMs will remain that have combined the ability to slash costs drastically while keeping the ability to create fascinating products. Again, the key to success is associ-ated with the product creation process. To respond to consumers' demands that are constantly increasing and diversifying, OEMs have widened their ranges of model lines, such as Mercedes with the A-series, V-series, M-series, and the SLK. In parallel, many OEMs also have increased the number of variants in order to be able to serve customers even better. This involves expenses that must somehow be accounted for. The cost savings associated with platform and carry-over concepts as well as standardization are not sufficient to cover this increase.

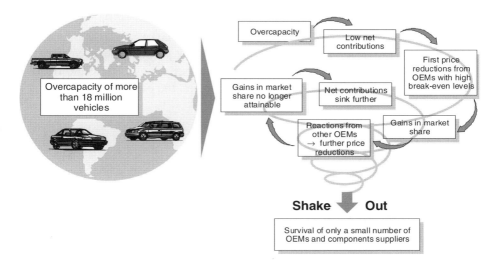

Figure 1   Worldwide excess capacity of more than 18 million units inevitably will lead to a global price war followed by a shakeout.

Even that is not enough. Fascination and a world of excitement are supposed to coax the customer, while a pleasant atmosphere in the interior, more comfort, greater safety, lower fuel consumption, and a competitive price are intended to convince the customer to buy. These challenges cannot be faced by walking on the usual path; they require developing new innovative approaches.

Merely developing new innovative vehicle concepts will not be enough. The vehicle development process must be totally restructured to avoid high expenditures caused by a variety of reasons. These include poor product quality resulting from inadequate testing, insufficient assessment of the development risk, delayed model introductions, slow production startups, production bottlenecks, and a general tendency for the last stages in testing a new model to be conducted by the customer. This is a very difficult task when you take into account different model lines, global platforms, regional variants, integration of globally operating modules and systems suppliers, modularity, and carry-over parts, etc. Another factor is gaining importance: time-to-market. This is the time from when a vehicle concept has been approved (the "styling freeze") until market introduction. This time must be within a range that approaches the limit set by the competition. Toyota, for instance, has set the benchmark at 15 months for Ipsum. From the viewpoint of the market, this is understand-able because the general conditions underlying the product specification are subject to the spirit and design trends of a time period, and "new and fresh" product features have a considerable influence on the purchase decision.

Innovation and Engineering Execution:
The Determinants of Success

As part of an integrated approach to product creation, innovation and engineering execution are the areas in which the key for mastering future challenges lies (Fig. 2).

Working on the assumption of "doing the right things (an innovative product) efficiently," the following paragraphs will outline the essential elements for successful innovation and engineering execution (Fig. 3).

The field of innovation has four core elements:

- Ability to generate innovative ideas
- A corporate climate that promotes innovation
- Identification of needs the customer has not yet articulated
- Investigation and selection of innovative product features

The objective in generating innovative ideas is to always keep a stock of practicable ideas on which new vehicle ranges can draw. Particular attention therefore should be devoted, of course, to those ideas that make possible a quantum leap in the dimensions of technology and customer benefit. The main prerequisite for the generation of new ideas is a corporate climate that allows innovative ideas to arise in all departments and be properly followed up.

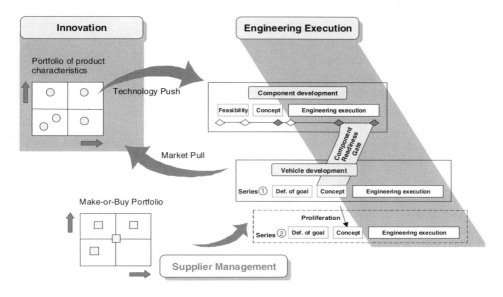

Figure 2   Integrative approach to product creation.

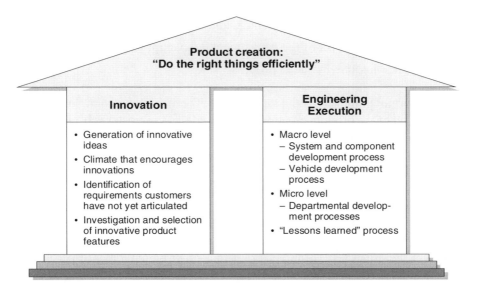

*Figure 3   Determinants for a successful survival strategy:
innovation and engineering execution.*

Even the best and most innovative ideas are of little use if they ignore the requirements of the customer target groups. Because years can lie between vehicle definition and market introduction, the identification of requirements that customers have not yet articulated also takes on great significance. Most final customers have great difficulty in specifying and articulating their future requirements without assistance.

If an OEM is successful in these disciplines, it ideally should have more innovative ideas available than can be implemented and financed. Because many of the decisions in the product creation process are basically intuitive, it is necessary to set up an objective framework of assessment for innovative concept approaches to guide screening. Basically, attention should be paid to ensuring that both the technocratic approach to the screening of ideas and a methodical overkill should be avoided because they would not be compatible with an innovative corporate climate.

While considering engineering execution, the second key success factor and one that leads to product cost reduction, three core elements must be taken into account:

- The macro level of the vehicle and component development process
- The micro level of the departmental development process
- The "lessons-learned" process

The important point here is the separation of the macro and micro levels. The macro level of the product creation process defines the master schedule, major milestones, and associated deliverables. It does not define how the deliverables and the required quality should be achieved. This is where the micro level process definition comes into the picture, (i.e., defining the processes for each participant or department that is participating in product creation). For example, the macro level defines that crash worthiness should be validated with the first prototype at time *xyz* and must fulfill certain specifications, whereas the micro level defines how to design the body in white or how to perform the crash test. Another point that must be emphasized here is the "lessons-learned" process, which should occur regularly at the end of every project or major phase. In many companies, the implementation of this process remains only rudimentary and does not receive high priority. However, this is the process that represents a central element in knowledge transfer and in the exploitation of optimization potential. If the present trends in the "learning organization" and knowledge management continue, this process will take on the priority it deserves.

Innovation: Generating Innovative Ideas

Although generating innovative ideas is a difficult business, most OEMs and component manufacturers have processes and institutions to identify new ideas and technologies, although they differ from one company to another. From the experience of Arthur D. Little, eight factors determine the success of a good idea-generating process:

- *Clear strategic guidelines*—The generation of suitable new ideas is virtually impossible if no clear guidelines exist regarding brand mission and strategic core themes. To be completely logical, every company needs a vision of its selected areas of growth and innovation, and therefore a clear definition of its strategic line of advance and priorities. This can be supported by four simple but essential questions:

  1. What are the values for which our company should stand?
  2. What products and services do we want to supply?
  3. What customer target groups would we prefer to serve?
  4. What significance should our products have for our customers?

- *Broad range of sources for new ideas*—Effective generation of ideas requires a large number of very different internal and external sources. When asked about sources for new ideas, many companies mention their internal suggestion schemes, under which employees are rewarded on the basis of the potential cost savings from their suggestions or the patents that can be obtained.

  To increase the chances of generating successful and pioneering new ideas, it is essential to break beyond the corporate boundaries and initiate an intensive exchange of ideas and joint activities with customers, suppliers, research organizations, industrial associations, etc. The requirement of confidentiality often is pushed as a reason for preventing such an exchange. In our opinion, in most cases this argument is used by those firms that have good ideas but can bring those ideas to the market only after a very long delay because of internal process problems.

- *Absolutely clear process management responsibilities*—The seamless generation of ideas requires clear lines of responsibility and duties. An important role is played by formal idea-collection processes such as brainstorming workshops, the administration of budgets for feasibility studies, research projects, and the connection with departments in the firm such as the intellectual property department. Depending on the organizational design, it is possible to imagine a department with its own budget and training facilities for innovation. However, it must be made clear that innovation is not the task of one dedicated department but one to be practiced by every operating department. Any other approach leads to isolation and thus to choking the pipeline of good ideas.

- *Methods and techniques for improving creativity and the flow of ideas*—In recent years, it has been possible to diagnose an explosion of creativity and stimulation techniques for generating ideas. With methods such as conceptual blockbusting, lateral thinking, and synectics, the flow of ideas can be increased to cause a "shift of paradigm" to occur. One approach that significantly improves the classic brainstorming approach in terms of quality, relevance, and speed is structured idea management. Figure 4 describes the process of how ideas are generated, assessed, and prioritized in several stages.

- *Resources for feasibility studies*—In many cases, the question of the feasibility of innovative ideas cannot be answered without further investigations into product concept and design, production process, or customer preference feasibility studies. Therefore, it makes sense to set aside special budgets for research and development projects or market surveys such as focus groups or "conjoint measurement," which can be made available to the departments doing the work at

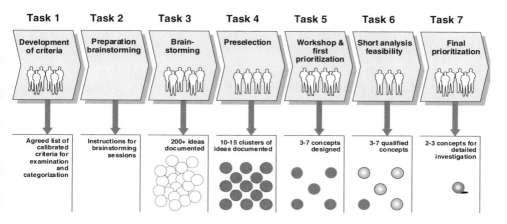

Figure 4 Structured idea management supports the generation of innovative ideas while taking full account of time and budget restrictions.

short notice and without administrative expense, but not necessarily within their own budget responsibilities.

- *Incentive systems*—To encourage employees to play a major role in the generation of ideas, a corporate climate that encourages innovation is vital. One important component of this is an adequate incentive and reward system. Many companies question the desirability of additional payments on the grounds that, for many employees in the product creation process, the generation of new ideas is part of their job descriptions. However, many measures can be taken to encourage and motivate employees without incurring major costs. Here are four examples:

  1. The head of the company creates an innovation prize.

  2. The recipients of patents are given rewards.

  3. The names of employees are published monthly (for instance, in the company newsletter), thanking them for making a significant contribution to the generation of ideas.

4. The generation of ideas forms a part of the annually agreed targets and can be included in the variable part of the employee's pay.

- *Measuring the effectiveness of the idea-generating process*— The seventh success factor deals with measurement of the effectiveness of the idea-generating process, in terms of success achieved. Measurements of success should be conducted periodically and can include both quantitative and qualitative dimensions, although these will differ considerably from one company to another. Examples of measurement dimensions are number of ideas, number of patents, number of ideas put into practice, and the percentage of profits from turnover with new products.

- *Standardized idea-generation process*—The basis for achieving these success factors is the existence of a standardized process for generating innovative ideas. This process must be transparent and comprehensible to every employee, meaning that it must be largely self-explanatory and should be able to work without administrative processes and without an excessive amount of detailed information.

Innovation: A Climate That Encourages Innovation

A structured and systematic idea-generating process may be important, but it will be totally ineffective if it does not occur within the context of a corporate climate that encourages innovation.

In a recent study by Arthur D. Little, in which nearly 700 companies participated from all over the world, more than 50 percent of those questioned in the motor industry were convinced that a corporate climate that encourages employees and rewards them for using their own initiative is a critical factor in the success of innovation. From of the viewpoint of these companies, a major challenge for increasing innovative product and process innovations consists in permanently overcoming "soft" cultural factors such as the "not invented here" syndrome. To establish how good or poor the performance of a company is with regard to important critical and cultural factors, Arthur D. Little developed the innovation climate sensor with which a company can compare itself with "best practice" (Fig. 5). To enable companies to refer to realistic and up-to-date benchmarks, opinion surveys have been carried out at regular intervals over the last 10 years.

The approach to creating an innovative climate thus does not consist of ambitious campaigns and activities that announce a new culture from "on top," but addresses the mechanisms in a company which, if they are not removed, condemn even the best-intended campaign to failure. This refers to the unwritten rules for which Arthur D. Little has developed an extensive analytical methodology. After the mainly informal mechanisms have been identified, appropriate steps for improvement can be defined and implemented.

The two most noticeable of all factors affecting innovation in the German motor industry can be described briefly here: fear of risk, and the "not invented here" syndrome. Fear of risk is understandable in the motor industry, because image and market value are heavily dependent on the customer retaining mobility without risk. One highly publicized example is the

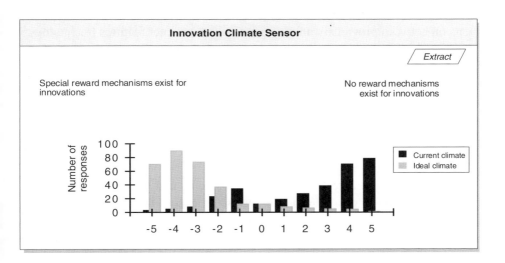

Figure 5   The Arthur D. Little innovation climate sensor identifies the performance of a company with regard to critical cultural factors.

A-series Daimler and its problems with the "moose test", where Daimler-Benz was able to prevent greater damage only by communicating swiftly and openly with the customer.

However, because new and innovative ideas are vital to the continued existence of a company, processes have to be established with the aid of which risks can be managed and minimized. The component parts of risk minimization begin at the selection procedure for the idea-generation process. Further information will be discussed here in detail in the section on engineering execution.

Innovation: Anticipation of Future Customer Requirements

Despite the declining position of the car as a status symbol, customers are demanding technically superior products that are individually tailor-made for their requirements, at shorter and shorter intervals. The strategy of placing largely standardized mass-produced products with high sales pressure is no longer sufficient for maintaining a position on the market. The ability to introduce customer-oriented vehicle models with innovations as a pioneer or quick follower in the market therefore is taking on vital significance in the motor industry. In particular, this ability consists in defining the right mix in the field of tension between previously unknown innovative product features (technology push) and market and customer requirements (market pull) in such a way that the vehicle will be neither too madly innovative nor a product that meets all customer needs but has no "sex appeal."

Most OEMs in the past have tended to move too far toward technology push, such as Daimler-Benz and BMW, or toward market pull, such as Opel and Ford. However, the decisive factor in success in the future will be an inwardly consistent concept that makes it possible to create a balanced field of tension between external market requirements and internal innovations. The aim will be to generate, on this basis, a product feature portfolio with which adequately to position each model range. To arrive at this creative field of tension, it will be necessary not only to fill the pipeline of ideas and innovations to the brim but also to possess excellent knowledge of the target groups and the market.

Some OEMs have now had the experience of seeing product features that arouse enthusiasm and affection only being mentioned occasionally in clinics. This is because the customer always tends to bring in the experience he has accumulated from the past and finds it difficult to articulate his future requirements and preferences. If one asks customers what they dislike about their vehicles, one has a chance of hearing points made in very clear language that otherwise reach only the managers in companies in a highly filtered form.

The identification of future customer requirements that cannot be articulated therefore is a task of the greatest importance, the successful handling of which can be expressed clearly in market share. The central key to this is the adequate analysis and segmentation of customer target groups, because this will more or less represent the foundations for the development of future requirement hypotheses.

Customer target groups and their characteristics—If customer target groups are not segmented correctly, the application of statistical processes such as layout measurement will degenerate into an expensive gambling game when these results later form the basis for positioning a vehicle.

Innovation does not have to be exclusively product-oriented, as can be seen from an innovative segmentation approach, which takes its line from the different values held by the various generations and derives from them the criteria that drive the vehicle purchase decision (Fig. 6). Ford has achieved pioneering successes by using this approach in the development of the F150 pickup truck and was able to increase its share of this vehicle market segment by almost 20 percent.

Innovation: Determination and Selection of Innovative Product Features

The art of the vehicle manufacturer lies in his ability to develop attractive product features within the field of tension between innovative ideas and customer needs and requirements. The following paragraphs will examine two processes in detail: the process of how to generate attractive features, and the process of how to select the best from among them.

	Personal Values	Values Relating to Cars
"Depression Kids" 1920–1934	Under the influence of the Depression and the World War, these children of the Depression make provisions for the future and always try to be on the safe side. They are also status conscious.	They prefer new models and change their cars every year. They choose long, low, wide, colorful vehicles. In their view, the right place for a truck is a building site or a farmyard.
"Quiet Generation" 1935–1945	Post-war childhood spent in peace and prosperity, a long innocent age. Few restrictions were imposed by their parents. Their favorite films idealize picaresque heroes.	They remember their past very clearly. They prefer very individual cars to attract attention. Trucks are accepted only for working purposes.
"Baby Boomers" 1946–1964	The first television generation. Their parents cosseted them, and this spurred them on to be successful. They look for instant rewards and want other people to regard them as astute buyers.	They regard a car as a "personality support." They buy mini-vans and SUVs to meet their requirement for comfort. The same applies to trucks and pickups.
"Lost Generation" 1965–1969	Deprived of their rights by growing up in the shadow of the Baby Boomers. They suffered from their parents' divorces, are not rich, and are only waiting for life to become better.	They drive small SUVs and niche models. They buy used cars because they cannot afford new ones.
"Birth Decline" 1970–1977	They grew up in the prosperous 1980s and thus developed relatively high standards, but their jobs do not allow them to satisfy those standards. They finally developed in a practical, focused, and future-minded direction.	They drive SUVs and practical station wagons. They consider a Jeep Wrangler to be a sports-minded car.
"Baby Boomlet" 1978–Present	The children of the Baby Boomers. They would like to be as prosperous as their parents' generation but will probably have to get by with less money.	Not yet fully developed. However, their generation will be nearly as large as that of their parents, and they will thus have a decisive influence on future products and marketing.

Figure 6 Generation-based target group segmentation (U.S.A.).

- *Generating relevant product features*—As part of the definition of a new model range, the innovative and product features connected with it take on great significance with regard to a durable differentiation from the competition. Anyone who in this situation can draw on intimate knowledge of the requirements of relevant target groups and a stock of innovative ideas from the idea-generation process will have placed himself in a favorable starting position.

One first step is the clustering of product features (Fig. 7) and the description of the ramifications of the product features on factors decisive to purchase (cross references), such as a comfort or safety and the selection of suppliers who take on a leading position (and are therefore called lead suppliers).

This process should not take place in a vacuum but in workshops in which various different departments participate: designers, developers, marketing specialists, etc. The next step is to check the data for plausibility and to form blocks of subjects with a clear reference to

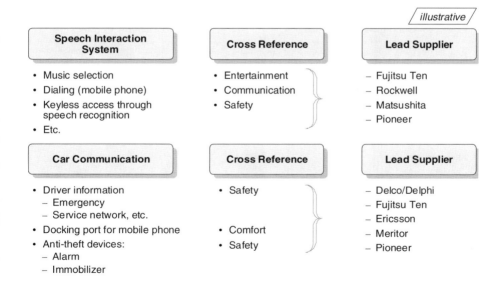

Figure 7 The first step toward the selection of innovative product features consists of identifying clusters, cross references, and lead suppliers.

strategically relevant aims—and backed with relevant arguments and data to justify selection of these features. The important point in this array of arguments and counter-arguments is that it should be drawn up on the basis of prescribed criteria which will simultaneously form the basis for later evaluation and selection.

- *Evaluation and selection of product features*—The methodology of evaluation is heavily dominated by the selection of the overall criteria. In the case of product features that are relatively independent of one another and have a clear product reference (e.g., automatically dipping interior mirrors), an evaluation based on the attractiveness and risk has proved to be a viable route. An important point here is the need to evaluate attractiveness and risk in strictly objective terms based on quantifiable individual criteria (Fig. 8). After all the product features have been evaluated for attractiveness and risk by an interdisciplinary team, they can be categorized into an appropriate portfolio and selected on the basis of a previously defined strategy of standards.

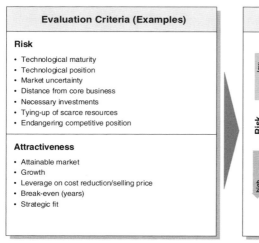 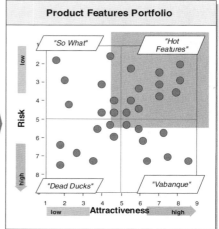

Figure 8 The evaluation and selection of product features are based on attractiveness and risk criteria.

When the desired excess supply of features has been achieved, the top right-hand square will be the first choice because these features combine the highest attractiveness with the lowest risk. However, features bearing a high risk should not be ruled out immediately but should be subjected in the appropriate individual cases to a deeper analysis of the risk assessment. Such product features should in any case be kept back has a potential reserve.

The product features thus discovered should find their way to so-called lead users before being placed in target catalogs or specifications so that an initial target-group validation can be performed. Lead users represent the prototype of an ideal customer who knows his future requirements exactly. On the one hand, these users are capable of showing enthusiasm and applying know-how with regard to new products and technologies. On the other hand, they also are value-for-money oriented and have a healthy feeling for trends. After an initial validation of the selected product features by lead users, product clinics then can be considered as a possible next step.

Engineering Execution

Within the product creation process in which approximately 70 percent of the product costs will already be determined, a significant number of cost drivers can be avoided if the process is designed properly. Experience shows that a few undesirable symptoms can be identified, such as the explosive increase in the number of changes shortly before series production starts, poor initial quality, missing parts and components, postponements of the start of production (SOP), enormous overruns on the development budget, and paralysis of the startup team because of constant "fire fighting."

These symptoms usually are attributable to general weakness in the process concept and/or to missing or deficient support processes such as quality assurance and risk management. In individual cases, weak and defective project management and/or unsuitable project organization also can be the cause. We do not intend, however, to go into any more detail at this point on the broad subject of project management.

To eliminate these symptoms, the product creation process must be restructured from its very foundations upward. Previous approaches usually began with the product definition and then worked their way forward in the direction of SOP. By trying to define product design in the very early development phases (vehicle definition and vehicle concept development), the phase of engineering execution usually is robbed almost entirely of any room for maneuver. A factor in success for competitiveness is thus the redesign of the processes starting at the back, with engineering execution, and working forward (Fig. 9).

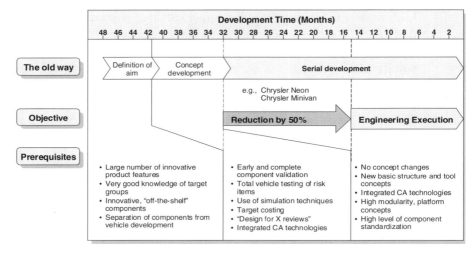

Figure 9   Restructuring the product creation process starts with engineering execution.

Here it is necessary to work out in detail and with precision the prerequisites for the engineering execution phase and the phases preceding it, and then to implement them. Although the length of time allocated to engineering execution is shorter than in the usual average development timetable, this does not necessarily have to apply to the concept and definition phase. The background to this is that, for instance, the concept phase is less subject to market forces in the sense of time-to-market than to the milestone dates in a vehicle manufacturer's overall model program planning.

Successful restructuring therefore starts at two levels for engineering execution. One level is the strategically orientated level (macro level) through which the development philosophy is operationalized. The second level is the micro level, which affects departmental work and the process in detail—so much so, in fact, that on this basis SAP and CAD/CAX systems can be used to support and automate the processes. The development time reduction must be synchronized on both levels.

Engineering Execution: Macro Level

When restructuring the macro level, attention should be paid to ensuring that the process concept is sturdily designed to prevent malfunctions and that it supports development philosophies such as front-loading. This includes the earliest possible confirmed validation of functionalities, quality, cost, process reliability, etc. in the subsystems, modules, and components—and at the same time a late freeze on the overall vehicle concept. This will prevent expensive changes and time-consuming delays in development later.

A further requirement for a short engineering execution phase is the separation of component development from overall vehicle development to minimize mutual obstructions and risks. This will mean that components such as motors and modules can be made available for a number of different model series simultaneously and thus display parallels to the platform concept in the model series.

The main factor in guaranteeing a successful engineering execution is discipline. It is also important to have support processes including, for instance, supplier management, review and risk management, and change management (Fig. 10). The following paragraphs describe three support processes, as examples in no particular order.

- *Support process: Supplier integration*—Cooperation and coordination among OEMs and suppliers is a particularly critical parameter because insufficient supplier integration will mean that cost reduction potential will be missed, and poor coordination will lead to higher change costs, particularly during series startup.

- *Support process: Design for X reviews*—This support process includes regular reviews by an experienced group that is not directly responsible for the creation of any specific model range. This support process likewise is an important instrument in all phases of

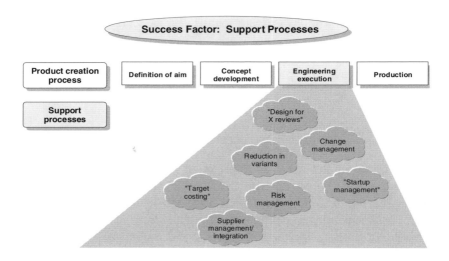

Figure 10   Successful product development requires the implementation of essential support processes.

product creation, although the priorities will differ considerably. The progress of product development will be reviewed at regular intervals on a number of dimensions such as product costs, production and assembly feasibility, ease of production and assembly, and testing feasibility. If major deviations emerge, the necessary measures will be agreed to and taken (Fig. 11).

Another important point is the simultaneous evaluation of design along multiple dimensions (design for X) because if conflicts arise, the obvious remedy that affects one dimension often has a negative effect on another dimension.

Support process: Target costing—Target costing has to be considered throughout all development phases. Target costing is a support process, the responsibility of which is to assure throughout the development process that the planned cost level is always maintained. This is not an easy task because the cost breakdown is quite complex and difficult to monitor.

Target costs usually are defined during the definition phase of a car using a top-down procedure. First, the price level is determined, one that fits to the positioning and the required volume of the model line. The total cost is

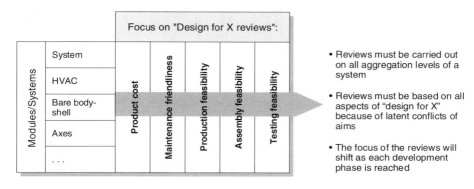

Figure 11   "Design for X reviews" should be conducted during the product creation process for all essential components.

derived from price by subtracting taxes, dealer margins, and the desired profit margin. In a further step, total costs must be split into overhead costs, nonrecurring costs (such as R&D costs or tooling), and recurring product costs. Total product costs also must be broken down to the component level.

During the concept phase, the main task is to find component designs that are in line with target costs. When the concept does meet the target costs, the only way to monitor costs during the engineering execution phase is to implement a robust engineering change process.

Engineering Execution: Micro Level

At the micro level, processes at the operational division or department level (such as vehicle development) are managed, and the resultant processes are synchronized with those at the macro level. As a result, three process groups are linked together:

- Operational processes, such as engineering execution in the suspension area
- Support processes, such as quality management
- Planning processes, such as the budget calculation

By harmonizing the individual processes in a sensible way, it is possible to shorten throughput times and reduce process costs because the process interfaces, as well as tasks and responsibilities, are defined and coordinated in a transparent manner. A prerequisite for this is adequate analysis and definition of the individual processes—a recognizable shortcoming in many companies. The prerequisite for synchronization is information from other process managers for use as the input to each individual process.

Various efficiency-increasing measures are possible. By reducing the interfaces involved in the process, throughput times can be reduced. Activities that do not contain any value creation, such as monitoring and coordination work, should be examined to see if they can be eliminated. The authority to make decisions should be delegated to the working level to minimize inspection and monitoring work. Basically, communication should be improved and processes standardized as much as possible. These measures often lead to a process-orientated reorganization of the company.

Substantial reductions in development times can be achieved only by those manufacturers that place targets and the principal solution at the macro level while at the same time having a "bottom-up" system at the micro level that shows whether and how this is possible. Synchronization between the two levels will not be a one-time process in reality, but an iteration process that brings the two levels closer to one another step by step. This process should be defined from the viewpoint of continuous improvement.

Engineering Execution: "Lessons-Learned" Process

The lessons-learned process has not been given much prominence in corporations. It is almost never adequately carried out and rarely finds its way into other departments or new projects. Toyota has an exemplary lessons-learned manual that creates the basis for transferring experience gained on previous projects (and particularly through design reviews) into new projects. Although great significance is accorded to the subjects of the learning organization and knowledge management, it is rare to find such a practical approach with a potentially great benefit. This is in stark contrast to many academic exercises in the field of knowledge management. Figure 12 shows one example of a lessons-learned process that is simple to implement.

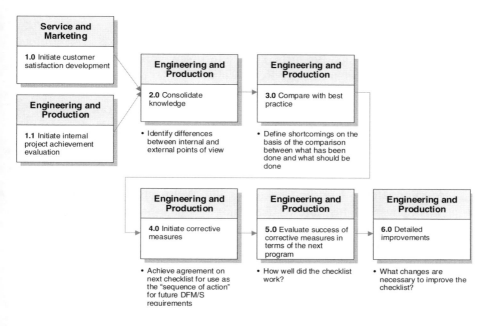

Figure 12   Lessons learned at the end of a vehicle project enable knowledge to be transferred to new projects.

Literature

"Knowledge Management—Reaping the Benefits, Second Quarter 1998," Arthur D. Little.

"Management von Innovation und Wachstum ("Management of innovation and growth"), Arthur D. Little, Gabler Verlag, 1997.

Feige, A., "Nur noch acht Systemintegratoren" (Only Eight System Integrators Left"), in *Automobil-Produktion*, June 1998, pp. 88–90.

Feige, A., and Walker, J., "World Class as Standard," in *Automotive International*, January 1998, pp. 48–49.

Feige, A., and Wolters, H., "Entwicklung: Der Schlüssel zum Überleben" ("Development: The Key to Survival"), in *Automobil Entwicklung—Design-Technologie*, September 1997, pp. 132–134.

Karsten, H., and Feige, A., "Projektmanagement," in Bühne, R. (Hg.), *Organisation*, Verlag Moderne Industrie, 1993/1994 (Loseblattsammlung).

Krauch, H., and Sommerlatte, T., *Bedürfnisse entdecken—Gestaltung zukünftiger Märkte und Produkte* ("Discovering Needs, Designing Future Markets and Products"), Frankfurt/New York, 1997.

Landmann. R., "Mitten in einer Revolution" ("In the Middle of a Revolution"), in *Autohaus* 11/98, pp. 18–20, 1998.

Scott-Morgan, P., *The Unwritten Rules of the Game*, New York, 1994.

Wolters, H., and Feige, A., "Änderungswut vor Serienanlauf" ("Wild Outburst of Changes Just Before Series Start-Up"), in *Automobil-Entwicklung*, May 1998, pp. 64–69.

Womack, J.P., Jones, D.T., and Roos, D., "Die Zweite Revolution in der Autoindustrie—Konsequenzen aus der Weltweiten Studie aus dem Massachussetts Institute of Technology" ("The Second Revolution in the Motor Industry—Consequences from the MIT Worldwide Study"), Frankfurt/New York, 1990.

Systems—A Revolution in Purchasing

Heiko Wolters

> *It is difficult to say what's impossible*
> *Because the dream of yesterday is the hope of today*
> *and the reality of tomorrow.*
> —Robert Goddard

Competitive pressure, especially from the Japanese vehicle manufacturers, has led to rethinking of the traditional structures and ways of working among European and American manufacturers in the last few years. The classic way of purchasing parts and components from numerous suppliers has been replaced by purchasing complex and often prefabricated systems. This form of purchasing generates numerous advantages for all those involved, especially related to costs, quality, and development time. This system of purchasing, however, also creates new demands on the competence of the companies as well as the type and form of cooperation among the vehicle manufacturers and their parts suppliers. The parts suppliers must be integrated into the vehicle development at an early stage, and new logistics concepts must be developed which ensure just-in-sequence delivery. This chapter describes two case studies that represent possible forms of cooperation.

A New Trend or a Temporary Phenomenon?

The disadvantage in productivity of the American and European automobile industries compared to Japanese companies at the end of the 1980s led to massive changes in the way products are developed, purchased, and produced. As a result, some companies were able to successfully increase their competitiveness again.

Bit by bit, materials purchase was discovered as a significant way of influencing an increase in profitability of companies. There is a good reason for this: Approximately 60 to 70 percent of the total work by vehicle manufacturers comes from expenses for materials, whereas only about a third of the added value is created internally (Fig. 1). Moderate cost savings in purchasing therefore create significant improvements in profits.

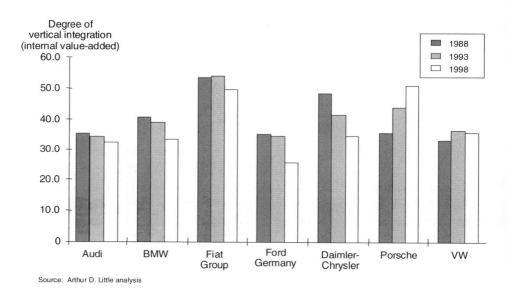

Source: Arthur D. Little analysis

Figure 1   Added value at OEMs.

The strategy of vehicle manufacturers both to increase the procurement volume and to purchase increasingly complex units that are sometimes already pre-assembled—so-called systems—has made an important contribution toward increasing efficiency in automotive firms. Although parts form the smallest units which are then assembled to form components, modular systems consist of several components that are joined so that pre-assembly is possible. Thus, for example, Daimler-Benz purchases a pre-assembled exhaust module for the current E Class which consists of a muffler, pipes, and a catalytic converter. In contrast to this, the functional systems are characterized by components working together. However, a functional system does not form a unit for assembly. For example, a braking system would include, in addition to brake pads and calipers, the brake cylinders and ABS. A mega-system consists of both modular and functional systems, extended with individual components. A wheel suspension mega-system, for example, would consist of the modular system spring strut as well as the functional braking system.

In early 1990s, the strategy of purchasing complete systems was only reluctantly put into place. The initial foray was largely limited to systems that were easy to delineate, such as seats or instrument panels. By now, the companies in the purchasing chain, both the vehicle manufacturers and the parts suppliers, have adjusted to the system strategy, so that the "new" methods have gained momentum and the scope of the systems purchase has broadened. We expect that this development will continue in the coming years.

What Are the Advantages for OEMs and Parts Suppliers?

Initially, suppliers were against system purchasing because it shifted the burden of performance without increasing compensation. However, with consistent implementation, both the vehicle manufacturer and the supplier have started to profit from system purchasing. The manufacturer obtains higher-quality, innovative products at lower prices and lower risk. The supplier benefits from an increased sales volume, a stable business relationship, and greater competitiveness.

For example, a comparison of the manufacturing costs for complete seats purchased in different ways shows that those made externally cost approximately 25 percent less than those produced in-house. If the supplier also is responsible for the development, then a savings of more than 30 percent is possible.

Significant rationalization effects can, however, be expected only when the vehicle manufacturer integrates the supplier partner early and consistently in the development of the vehicle and the partner is able to work effectively with the manufacturer. The vehicle manufacturer can profit from the development and innovation know-how of the supplier in two ways.

In the phase before concept definition, the OEMs and the selected systems suppliers can jointly rethink the traditional system limitations and approaches, and they may come up with completely new proposals for cost and use optimization. Thus, during the development of the cockpit system for the Chrysler Dakota, for example, the support for the dashboard was constructed so that in addition to its traditional support function, it also would serve as an air duct. This makes additional air duct parts superfluous, leading to the corresponding advantages in cost and weight.

The second way in which the manufacturer benefits is to realize the "design-to-cost" potential. For example, when the supplier adapts the design of the system to his manufacturing conditions, as well as to his parts program, costs can be reduced by using identical parts in different units. The supplier can accelerate the intensive process of identifying the problem and its solution, thereby reducing the number of alterations. This results in faster vehicle development times. As an example, without the early integration of parts suppliers in the development, the 24-month development time constraint for the Audi A3 would never have been met.

In reality, the working relationship between manufacturers and parts suppliers is never entirely smooth. The daily development work does not allow the partners to delineate each task or make those tasks entirely transparent. The resulting redundancies and iterations lead to a loss of efficiency in the work processes. If a halfhearted integration in the development process takes place, for example, without adequate consensus on the cost target, with only a rudimentarily defined product scope and contents, a significant cost overrun occurs. The supplier can recover the costs at a later time only with numerous part changes induced by the OEM (Fig. 2).

In terms of purchasing, the vehicle manufacturer profits from a reduced number of suppliers. The number of direct suppliers can be reduced by procuring systems—instead of parts and components—which also reduces administrative expense and releases resources for other tasks. At the same time, the quantity of parts numbers can be reduced. The supplier profits from volume effects of "single sourcing," because the system cannot be divided deliberately among various suppliers due to the high material and overhead investments involved.

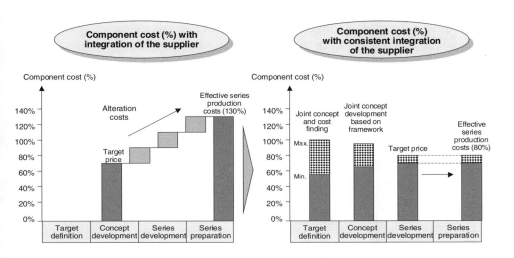

Figure 2   Supplier integration.

Beyond that, the just-in-sequence delivery of the systems means that there is no need to maintain any stocks close to the production line, which in turn reduces the capital requirements. In addition, less space is required in the factory because the systems often are delivered pre-assembled. The vehicle manufacturer profits from completely pre-assembled systems because this reduces the quality assurance measures.

What Are the Limitations of the System Concept?

With the implementation of the system concept, vehicle manufacturers have been able to continually reduce their number of parts and component suppliers in the last few years. At the same time, some selected system suppliers have been allowed to deliver a greater range of products as long as they assume a greater responsibility for their development. This process has gained momentum because it is reinforced by the activities of the supplier companies.

A few years ago, side paneling, middle consoles, seats, instrument panels, or dash panels were independent functional systems of the interior. Now the interior is a system produced by firms such as Lear, Johnson Controls, and Magna. The competence of the suppliers has increased so much that they can produce systems of enormous complexity. The current two largest seat manufacturers of the past, Lear Corporation and Johnson Control, have acquired various companies in the last few years to implement their mega-system strategy for the entire vehicle interior (Fig. 3).

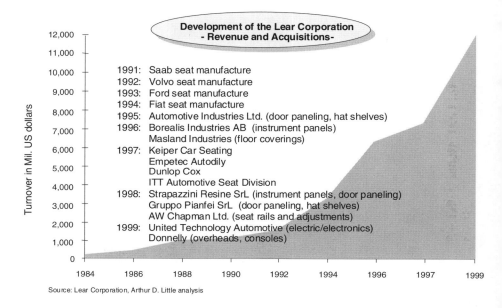

Source: Lear Corporation, Arthur D. Little analysis

Figure 3   Takeovers in the interior area.   Example: The Lear Corporation.

Similar developments are starting to occur in other product areas. Thus, complete front ends consisting of lighting, radiator, and bumpers are being offered as mega-systems by the French supplier ECIA and by the German company Hella. Brose supplies complete door systems to Volkswagen for the Passat. The Chrysler Jeep receives complete braking systems from ITT, consisting of ABS, brake calipers, servo-boosters, cylinders, disks, and pads. The American supplier Dana even supplies a complete rolling chassis for DaimlerChrysler. With this background, it is appropriate to ask what the limitations of these developments are and how large the systems may become in the future.

The limit as to how large the systems eventually will become cannot be defined universally because the answer depends both on the purchasing strategy and the production capabilities of the vehicle manufacturer, as well as on the availability of competent suppliers. In the long term, it is possible that nearly the entire vehicle, especially one targeted to a specific niche, may come from the hands of an integrating system supplier. The "manufacturer," whose brand name is on the product, merely assumes the responsibility for the overall project, the definition of the vehicle design, and the coordination.

Truck production by Volkswagen in Brazil can be seen as a first step in this direction. Here, system suppliers are responsible for complete assembly of the vehicle in the plant (see the following case study for details). General Motors is even going one step further with the Blue Macaw small-car project currently under development in Brazil. In this case, in addition to the assembly work, GM also awards significant development duties to the system suppliers who in turn control their subcontractors. General Motors is merely responsible for the overall vehicle design and the coordination of the system suppliers. Cost savings of an average of 30 percent are expected from this form of cooperation.

Case Study*:
Volkswagen Resende, Brazil

One of the most interesting examples for system sourcing is the Volkswagen plant in Resende, which is 150 km from Rio de Janeiro. Approximately 60 trucks (7 to 35 tons) and 15 bus chassis are produced daily in this plant. (Volkswagen has about 20 percent of the Brazilian truck market.)

Conceived by José Ignacio López de Arriortúa, the former purchasing director and executive at Volkswagen, the Resende plant was unveiled in November 1996 under the slogan "The automobile plant of the 21st century—A breakthrough in traditional automobile manufacturing." It has a planned daily capacity of 120 vehicles.

---

* The author thanks Kai-Uwe Hirschfelder for his valuable contributions to this case study.

In this first and only plant by Volkswagen for medium-sized trucks, a new philosophy for production and purchasing was implemented. In the concept known as "Consórcio Modular," all suppliers work together under one roof and manufacture the final product. Each of the systems suppliers monitors a modular system consisting of an assembly area, a warehouse area, and its own delivery ramp. Each is therefore responsible for its own logistics, workplace design, and assembly. On the other hand, Volkswagen is responsible for plant management, product development, quality assurance, customer service, and parts purchasing from third parties. From the total of 1,000 employees, only 200 are Volkswagen staff. In comparison, a traditional truck plant of this size has approximately 2,500 employees.

To support the team concept, all employees of the suppliers and Volkswagen wear the same working clothes; only the company logo on the breast pocket indicates for whom they actually work. Equally, the wage structures of the employees within the same category of activity are uniform, which made cooperation with unions possible on a consensus basis.

Only one Volkswagen employee, the so-called "maestro," is involved in the assembly of each vehicle. He accompanies the individual steps in the assembly process and is responsible for quality assurance. The direct customer orientation is taken into account because the name of the maestro and his telephone number are entered into the vehicle documentation, making him the contact person for the customer should any questions arise.

Every morning, the representatives of the seven system suppliers and the plant directors from Volkswagen meet at a roundtable discussion. There they deal with the fine planning for the production and jointly make important decisions for the daily business.

Control and cooperation with subcontractors is coordinated by the system suppliers. The seven integrated system suppliers assemble both parts and components they produce themselves, as well as those purchased from subcontractors (Fig. 4):

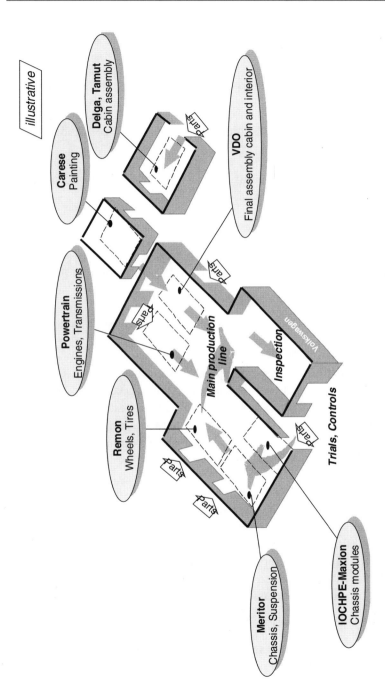

Figure 4 Layout of the Volkswagen Resende plant.

- The chassis module supplier **IOCHPE-Maxion** assembles the fuel tank, ducts, cabling, air tank, and steering.

- The axle manufacturer **Meritor** assembles the suspension, springs systems, and brakes.

- The service company **Remon** assembles the wheels and tires from various manufacturers.

- Powertrain, a joint venture by **MWM** and **Cummins**, builds and installs engines and transmissions.

- The company **Carese** operates the Eisenmann paint plant.

- **Delga** supplies the cabin framework. The stampings are made in the Delga plant in São Paulo and are welded together in the Resende plant.

- The instrument panel maker **VDO** is responsible for the entire interior of the cabin.

The payment of the system suppliers occurs only when the finished truck or finished bus chassis has successfully passed the last stage of assembly (Point 7) and has passed a general test of function. This ensures that each system supplier installs only components that function perfectly because payment of those suppliers depends on the functioning of the entire vehicle.

A partnership approach with the suppliers also was followed with investments. Thus, the system suppliers had to finance a total of 50 million U.S. dollars from the total investment of 300 million U.S. dollars. Although Volkswagen is the owner of the factory building, the suppliers are the owners of the machines and equipment it houses. Financial interdependence—for example, with reference to the distribution of profits or the assignment of losses—does not exist.

Volkswagen was able to profit from the Consórcio Modular in various ways:

- Significant cost savings potentials could be achieved through efficient logistics and lowered personnel expenses.

- The inclusion of the suppliers reduced the refinishing work and improved quality.

- The high degree of flexibility of the production process enables special customer wishes, for example, special wheelbases, to be taken into account with little preparation time.

After overcoming initial problems, the Consórcio Modular is a success from the viewpoints of both Volkswagen and the suppliers.

New Structures of Cooperation

The system strategy concept will lead to completely new structures, both for OEMs and for suppliers. The complexity of products will lead to increased demands on the part of the suppliers. The vehicle manufacturers will concentrate their core competencies on development, whereas suppliers will assume full responsibility for design, production, coordination of subcontractors, functionality, and quality for the entire system. Because this complex performance cannot be accomplished by any one supplier, a network of suppliers that work with each other under the guidance of a global system integrator will be created.

The project management competencies of the system integrator will be a critical success factor. The integrator will need to be in close contact with the OEM, while coordinating an efficient global purchasing network. The system integrator also acts as a development consultant for the OEM—one that has a broad range of technological and material know-how and ability to offer solutions to issues that the OEM may face.

For the synchronous production (just-in-time) and the synchronous delivery (just-in-sequence) to work properly, the logistics must ensure the availability of materials. In addition, the complex and often pre-assembled systems are difficult to stack and therefore are difficult to transport. The classic solution to the transportation issues—having suppliers locate within a few kilometers of the vehicle assembly plant—is no longer efficient. Although this would shorten the delivery distance, the cost-intensive loading and unloading and the necessary forklift traffic would remain.

As a result, system suppliers will have to locate on the plant premises of the vehicle manufacturer. Also, local assembly will become the norm. Audi in Ingolstadt, Germany, supports this, for example, with an industrial park located just outside the plant gate, which offers suppliers the entire infrastructure—from rail platforms to a container station and transportation to IT systems. Logistics costs can be reduced by approximately 30 percent through reduced freight, container, and handling expenses. In Rastatt, Germany, where the Mercedes A Class is made, the suppliers are linked to the final assembly via a conveyor—without any intermediate storage. An additional bonus is increased flexibility created by a reduction in the lead time required for production planning.

An alternative to this is local assembly in which the supplying companies complete the systems in the plant of the vehicle manufacturer. The logistics costs are then reduced to a minimum because the transport and packaging are almost completely unnecessary. At DaimlerChrysler, for example, Lear Corporation produces complete seat systems for the Mercedes SLK Roadster. Krupp/Hoesch makes complete axles for the Boxster on the plant premises of Porsche.

Another possibility is that a new form of suppliers might arise to handle all logistics requirements of the vehicle manufacturer. Regardless of the location of the supplier, the logistics service company ensures that the necessary materials arrive at the OEM on time. This can go so far that the vehicle manufacturer merely needs to transmit the vehicle sales figures to the logistics service company, which then would take care of the entire purchasing logistics, starting with the order scheduling and going all the way to delivery. The logistics concept of the Saturn plant of General Motors in Tennessee, U.S.A., is moving in this direction. There, the service company Ryder handles the entire purchase logistics. (See the following case study for details.)

Case Study:
The Saturn Plant and Integrated Logistics Management

In the early 1980s, General Motors (GM) started the Saturn project to develop and produce innovative small vehicles. The goal of the project was to counter the increasing import pressure by the Japanese and to improve the relationship with the United Auto Workers (UAW). The traditional approaches and methods therefore were rethought and replaced with new forms of cooperation.

A team charged with developing concepts inspected the more than 100 vehicle plants of General Motors and competitors with regard to "best practices." The result of the analysis was identification of several factors important to the success of a company. These include consistent orientation toward internal and external customers, mutual trust between the unions and management, employees being responsible for their own work, and a partner relationship with suppliers. These factors were put into practice at Saturn.

The Saturn plant was built in 1989. It was located on an area of 500 million square meters in Tennessee and required a total investment of 1.9 billion U.S. dollars. In the following summer, the first vehicles rolled off the assembly line. Today Saturn produces four-door sedans (S and L Series) and a coupe. In the J.D. Power customer satisfaction analysis, Saturn remains the undisputed Number One American vehicle manufacturer.

The philosophy of partnership which characterizes the activities of Saturn is also the cornerstone of the relationships with suppliers. This is based on mutual trust, high quality, just-in-time delivery, and continuous improvement.

A new and innovative concept was put into practice for the purchasing logistics. Instead of managing the inbound and outbound logistics itself, Saturn decided to use an integrated logistics service company. The company Spring Hill Integrated Logistics Management (ILM), a subsidiary of Ryder Systems, is solely responsible for the delivery of production materials for the entire vehicle assembly, as well as the delivery of the vehicles to the more than 360 dealer locations.

On the purchasing side, ILM handles not only the pickup of completed purchases from approximately 326 suppliers, but also the coordination of suppliers and inspection. Depending on the parts, they are then either sent directly to the assembly line or, after brief intermediate storage in a warehouse near the plant, are fed into the production cycle at the proper sequence to arrive just-in-time within a five-minute window of delivery. The orders for the suppliers are triggered at Saturn by withdrawal principle similar to Kanban, with corresponding notification to the logistics specialist.

More than 450 deliveries with 1,800 transactions are handled in this way every day. Saturn offered a four-year contract in which ILM is paid not by trip or quantity delivered, but by the number of vehicles produced. Saturn has managed to substantially reduce logistics costs by this form of cooperation.

Before a supplier can deliver mega-systems, it must acquire the technology and materials competence necessary for the product development process and be able to manage the coordination of the product/performance package as well as the series production. These obstacles become even more formidable when the resources are to be made available on a global scale.

This means that the critical size for a Tier-1 supplier in the future will be significantly larger than that found today. The financial sophistication required to provide systems on a global scale is fairly significant. In addition, the human resources required to meet the future vision are much different than those available today. It will not be enough to perfect one's own techniques and materials. What will be needed is management performance—from the process control (say, as part of simultaneous engineering) up to coordination of numerous subcontractors and partners in the cascading supplier pyramid of the future.

New structures also will be necessary on the part of the vehicle manufacturers. The classic form of cooperation in which the supplier executes only according to rigid guidelines will be replaced by cooperation among partners. The greater integration of the system partners and the transfer of extensive performance packages and responsibilities will lead to new company processes and a new organizational structure. This will include:

- Temporary places of work for selected developers from the suppliers—so-called resident engineers—will be set up by the vehicle manufacturers to simplify their integration in the development processes, to make communication channels shorter, and to improve coordination.

- Central contact persons—so-called sponsors—will be set up for the systems suppliers by the vehicle manufacturers. Thus, a supplier of brake systems works with various departments of the manufacturer, for example, in the development of the chassis, the development of the electronics, and the overall vehicle development. Because these departments often do not follow coordinated goals, the sponsor can function as a central coordination center for the suppliers.

- The samples will not only be made available by the system partners, but will be installed and inspected jointly with the vehicle manufacturer. This will make causes of failures and dependencies among installed components understandable for the suppliers and will increase the degree of maturity of the vehicle.

- Risk and opportunities will be shared more than in the past among suppliers and vehicle manufacturers using "risk-sharing configurations." This includes the distribution of investment risks in machines and locations, the one-time costs of development, costs for recalls, and field failures or earnings from sales. In addition, suppliers integrated in planning and development will participate financially from reductions or increases in development costs, weight reductions, or time delays.

Outlook

The increased demands on supplier companies will lead to a major reduction in the supply base. Only a few suppliers will be able to become systems integrators, as can be judged by reviewing the following checklist. This does not, however, necessarily mean that the remainder of the companies will disappear from the market. Niche specialists and subcontractors will continue to exist in the future. The intensity of competition and the associated rivalry will increase, however, and the future existence of a supplier will depend on the appropriateness of the selected strategy.

Checklist for Potential System Integrators

1. Does our product play an important role from the viewpoint of the customer in a possible system?

2. Do we have the necessary project management competency and the corresponding resources to coordinate various subcontractors?

3. Do we have critical development and technology know-how to offer complete solutions to problems?

4. Do we have the necessary infrastructure, in terms of processes, production capacity, or cooperation partners?

5. Do we have the logistics competency and information management connections to supply just-in-sequence?

6. Do we have adequate financial strength to provide financing for complex development projects?

7. Do we have an excellent reputation with customers as a supplier of high-quality products?

8. Can we differentiate ourselves adequately from our competitors with our product-service offer?

Although approximately 10,000 Tier-1 suppliers existed in Europe in the early 1970s, according to internal estimates by Arthur D. Little, by the year 2005 only 350 such suppliers will exist in the future, which will include approximately 20 to 30 global integrators of mega-systems. This concentration process also will continue at the next level down. Some supplier companies will be taken over by larger companies and some will withdraw from the automotive market; others will not be able to withstand competitive pressures and will disappear from the market. Suppliers with a strongly diversified product range—without a clear strategic direction—will have difficulties withstanding competitive pressures remaining in the position of a Tier-1 supplier.

The speed with which the new system purchasing concepts are introduced, considering the need to make structural changes, will depend on the position that the vehicle manufacturers take, based on their will to change and their specific situation. In countries with strong unions, for example, there will be a need to develop consensus before a change of this magnitude can occur. The OEM also will need to decide what to do with pre-assembly areas that now become unnecessary. A solution that has been used in the past is to sell the assembly areas to suppliers. For example, DaimlerChrysler sold its plastics production to the French supplier Sommer Alibert.

The OEM must walk a tightrope. It has to find a balance between creating partnerships with a few systems suppliers while simultaneously keeping competition alive among the suppliers. The partnering companies, OEM, and system supplier depend on each other similarly to the links in a chain: the weakest link becomes the bottleneck and undermines the functioning of the entire system.

Literature

Baldwin, C.Y., and Clark, K.B., "Managing in an Age of Modularity," in *Harvard Business Review*, September–October 1997, pp. 84–93.

Karsten, H., Wolters, H., and Thorwirth, A., "Der Systemintegrator wird kommen," in *Automobil-Produktion*, October 1995, Landsberg, pp. 54–55.

Kleinaltenkamp, M., and Wolters, H., "Die Gestaltung von Systempartnerschaften zwischen Automobilherstellern und ihren Zulieferern—Eine spieltheoretische Analyse," in Schreyögg, G., and Sydow, J. (Hg.), *Gestaltung von Organisationsgrenzen*, Berlin/New York, 1997, pp. 45–78.

Lamming, R., *Beyond Partnership: Strategies for Innovation and Lean Supply*, London, 1993.

Nishiguchi, T., *Strategic Industrial Sourcing: The Japanese Advantage*, Oxford, 1994.

Wolters, H., *Modul- und Systembeschaffung*, Wiesbaden, 1995.

Wolters, H., and Schuller, F., "A Conceptual Framework for Optimizing the Assembler-Supplier Relation with System Sourcing—The Case of the German Automobile Industry," International Motor Vehicle Program Research Paper, Massachusetts Institute of Technology, Cambridge, MA, 1994.

Womack, J.P., and Jones, J.T., *Lean Thinking*, New York, NY, 1996.

Success Through Strong Brands— The Multi-Brand Strategy of the Volkswagen Group

Berthold Krüger

> *The marketing battle will be a battle of brands, a competition for brand dominance. Businesses and investors will recognize brands as the company's most valuable assets. This is a critical concept. It is a vision about how to develop, strengthen, defend, and manage a business...It will be more important to own markets than to own factories. The only way to own markets is to own market-dominant brands.*
> —Larry Light

Successful brands have a special charisma, a certain aura that transforms them into strong brands.

It is indisputable that good products are needed to achieve success, especially in the automobile industry. However, enough examples exist to prove that it is brand strength alone that determines success or failure when products offer comparable technology. Today, the Volkswagen Group has a portfolio of nine strong brands which are presented as individual personalities in the multi-brand strategy. This chapter will describe and explain the context and the elements of this multi-brand strategy.

1. The Volkswagen Group Around the World

The Volkswagen (VW) Group has continued to gain new momentum. 1999 was a good sales year for the group: 4.86 million cars were sold, 6 percent more than in 1998 and even more than ever in the past. Every ninth registered motor vehicle in the world is one of the VW Group's models, and the group's world market share is now 12 percent, up from 11.7 percent in 1998.

In Western Europe, one of the most important sales market, the VW Group was able to expand its passenger car market share to 18.9 percent. Volkswagen is on the way to regaining its old strength in North America as well. This is documented by the sales figures—more than 553,500 cars were sold in 1999, a gain of 32.0 percent over 1998, making it the best annual result since 1974.

2. Challenges for Sales and Marketing

The global auto market currently is undergoing a drastic period of change. The boundaries among national markets are disappearing, and information transparency is increasing at tremendous speeds, as is the rate of technical development.

We understand globalization to mean not only a single world market, but also an approach to appreciating customers' ways of life and attitudes around the world. The rapidly increasing number of Internet users is accelerating world-wide information transparency and international dialog. The number of Internet connections will grow from 55 million in 1998 to more than 150 million in the year 2000. Throughout the world, more than 100,000 connections are added every day. The Internet is an invitation to a spontaneous exchange of opinions, and what are known as communities are coming into being—small fragmentary groups that exchange views worldwide.

Increasing fragmentation is the greatest challenge facing the automobile industry (Fig. 1). Our analyses show that in 1987, customers perceived the market in terms of nine different vehicle segments. Within ten years, this number nearly tripled. In 1997 already, 26 different vehicle segments were perceived, and by next year, the trend toward design models will increase this number to more than 30. Roadsters, sedans, and sport utility vehicles, to name only a few examples, one day will be available in all size categories.

The fragmentation of the automobile market inevitably leads to a reduction in brand loyalty because customers are constantly being tempted by offers to try new vehicles and brands.

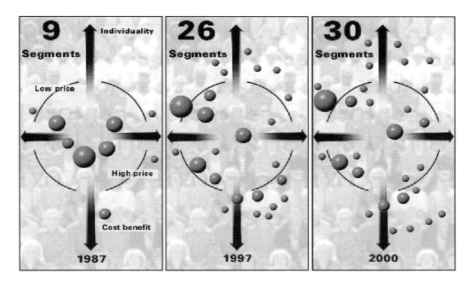

Figure 1   Fragmentation of markets.

Volkswagen's three-liter car is a good example of the rapid pace of technological development that reigned at the end of the 20th century. It is the first full-specification automobile that has room for four passengers and their luggage and that allows them to travel in comfort while using only three liters of gasoline per 100 kilometers.

The vehicle is not merely an example of technical perfection. It reflects an awareness of obligations toward society and the challenges of the future.

Motor racing influenced a series of development by automobile manufacturers in the past. Today, new technologies such as the three-liter automobile are decisively controlling the development of future generations of vehicles. The selective injection technology used in the three-liter TDI engine represents the state of the art in diesel engineering and is already used in many Volkswagen vehicles today.

Finally, the new information technologies, especially the Internet, will fundamentally change the use of automobiles in the form of car multimedia and the latest telematics applications.

3. The Volkswagen Group's Multi-Brand Strategy

The fast-living world of permanent change demands signposts that are provided through the value system of strong brands. The Volkswagen Group's brands provide signposts in this dynamic environment and represent values that are identical throughout the world. The multi-brand policy with its precise positioning of the individual brands serves as a basis for a global market strategy with a wide product range in all segments and markets.

Three components define the parameters of a multi-brand strategy:

- Global orientation of the brands' product characteristics with the goal of complete market coverage

- Clear brand positioning through the creation of brand personalities with emotional content

- Consistency and credibility of the brand experience from the product all the way through the marketing process

Global Alignment of the Product Policy

Figure 2 shows the segmentation of the passenger vehicle world market by size categories and body types, and in each case, as an example, the coverage until now by products from the individual group brands.

The number of segments is being extended continuously through the division of existing segments into further subsegments—for example, the off-road segment into classical user-oriented all-terrain vehicles and the leisure-oriented all-terrain vehicles derived from passenger car platforms. A large number of fields remain unoccupied, and the Volkswagen Group will develop those where sufficient demand exists.

The high-end segment of luxury sedans and sports cars has been covered by our purchase of Rolls-Royce, Bentley, Lamborghini, and Bugatti. With one stroke, we were able to successfully establish ourselves in this segment.

At the other end of the vehicle spectrum, we entered the compact car market with products such as the Seat Arosa and the VW Lupo. By the way, this

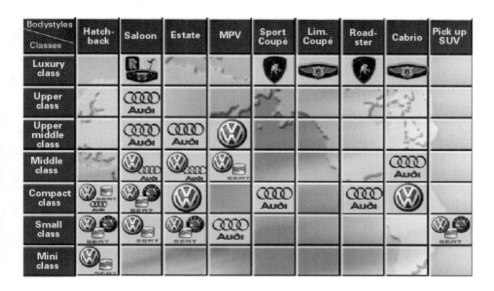

Figure 2   Segmentation of the global car market.

segment currently has the highest growth rates in Europe. We also estimate that more than 100,000 small cars can be sold in China each year, most of them to the growing numbers of private customers.

Thus, our goal must be to offer each customer the automobile that corresponds to his or her individual needs and lifestyle. This development continually results in new niche segments. You could almost say that the mainstream has become the sum of all of these niches. The Volkswagen Group has responded by offering new, emotionally charged vehicles such as the New Beetle, the Audi TT Coupé, the TT Roadster, and the Audi Allroad. At the same time, the various brands must cover different focuses of demand to minimize cannibalization effects within the group.

Maintaining the independent identity of the respective brand is a challenge. Therefore, we must surround our brands with a special radiance extending beyond the mere usefulness of the product—say, an aura—while at the same time continuing their further development. You can achieve this not only by the brand-specific design of the bodywork types and a differentiating pricing policy, but mainly through the unequivocal positioning of the brands and the creation of brand personalities with emotional fascination.

Clear and Precise Positioning of the Brands

Every brand represents a mission in the overall image of the Volkswagen Group, which is based on the roots of its origins and has been developed systematically into a comprehensive personality with values. This presupposes a process of continuous reflection about brands and markets.

First and foremost is the fact that the authenticity of the brand's image is retained at all times (Fig. 3), and the model is reflected in the actual product and marketing policy. If the substance of the products does not correspond to the brand's claims, then the foundation is missing and the brand loses its credibility. This applies to the automobile industry more than to all other industries.

Since early 1919, Bentley has stood for the serendipitous symbiosis of sportiness and luxury. The Bentley is the quintessential gentleman's sporting tourer.

Figure 3   Brand missions.

The achievements of the Bentley Boys, a group of young men from the best British families whose Le Mans wins in the 1920s were legendary, go unforgotten. They are ever present—not because of their victories but because of the heroic circumstances under which they took place. It may be mentioned in passing that these boys lived exciting but decidedly short lives. Only a few reached the age of 35, and none died a natural death, which of course contributed enormously to the establishment of the brand's legend.

The gap between the glorious past of the Le Mans victories and the present is bridged with the study of the Bentley Hunaudières, which celebrated its world premiere at the 1999 Automobile Salon in Geneva. The brand's mission corresponds to the Bentley Boys' motto, "Who dares, wins!"

The concept of sporting character, albeit in another embodiment, leads to the next new brand in the group: Lamborghini. Because of his dissatisfaction with his Ferrari, Ferruccio Lamborghini decided in 1963 to build a better sports car. Within only four years, he succeeded in realizing his aim. The Miura set new standards for driving performance and design in the 1960s. Today, the Diablo GT is the fastest series production sports car in the world. This car clearly embodies the central theme of the Lamborghini brand: "The ultimate force in sports cars."

Rolls-Royce was always the motor car of the crowned heads of this world—a jewel of automobile construction and the icon of luxury pure and simple.

Finally, Bugatti combines aesthetics and perfection with absolute exclusivity. "The masterpiece of automotive design and engineering" therefore is the mission of a brand whose founder, Ettore Bugatti, knew not only how to design motor cars but also how to create timeless masterpieces of automotive art. We are taking up this tradition again and leading it into the next millennium with the EB 218, the Chiron, and the Veyron.

These brands are surrounded with legends. They are enshrined in a mythology.

The Volkswagen brand also succeeded in doing this in the past with one product. As a synonym for Volkswagen, the Beetle stands for the democratization of mobility, confidence in the future, and the economic miracle in Germany. In the United States, it came to represent an entire generation.

The Golf continued this tradition and has long since achieved a cult status. It is a car that reflects the values of a global generation, a generation that could not be more varied but is united by one thing: driving a Golf. For this reason, we have named it Generation Golf.

However, it has been a long time since the Golf alone characterized the image of Volkswagen. Now it is joined by a variety of quality products—from the Lupo to the Passat. In particular, high standards, innovation, and a passion for perfection that reaches down to the smallest detail define the concrete implementation of the brand image through the product.

The Volkswagen brand defines the mission of setting new standards for building automobiles and of achieving the broadest possible coverage of nearly all market segments while doing so as the "Benchmark for automotive values."

Audi uses visionary technology and design to question convention. "The challenge to convention" is the mission of a brand that has staked its place among big automobile brands using pioneering technical achievements and extravagant design. With the Quattro drive system, Audi has set a historic milestone in motor vehicle technology. The continuing development of the brand from its roots to the present day shows the extravagant award-winning design of the Audi TT Roadster and Coupé.

Skoda can look back over a strong tradition of reliable and elegant vehicles as few other automobile brands can do. With its slogan "Creative solutions for smart customers," Skoda offers high-quality automobiles such as the Octavia at attractive prices.

The Seat brand combines Spanish temperament with German engineering efficiency. The Seat brand's new brand appearance with sporty emotional vehicles such as the Toledo and the Bolero and Formula concept studies clearly shows the brand's mission: "Automotive joy of life—puts the joy back into motoring."

Implementation of the central themes defined in the multi-brand strategy requires an ongoing process. The missions of the brands and the description of their images are target values that are implemented using the most diverse marketing tools.

In pricing, all of the brands follow the principle of the price-value strategy. This means that even with the group's volume brands, it is not primarily a question of offering the lowest possible prices but also of offering features that are appropriate to the brand as well. This is how the most attractive price-equivalent value ratio is created in practice. To ensure that an attractive value is provided, a corrected price index is created to provide a comparison with competing models on an equivalent basis. Thus, on a list price basis, the Golf is 10 percent more expensive than the average competition; however, when you consider what you get for that price, the corrected price is only 3 percent higher.

More than for any other product, an automobile is judged by its life cycle cost which includes maintenance costs, insurance costs, and resale value.

Here, the Volkswagen brand in particular is the leader in the competitive environment. This offering is important to private customers, but it is increasingly becoming the decisive criterion in the fleet business, whose traditional characteristic tended rather to be an aggressive discounting behavior.

Of course, the consistency and credible staging of the brand personalities is not limited solely to the product, but extends to the whole marketing chain in the automobile trade. This includes the system of exclusive distribution channels, the brand corporate identity, and the creation of brand "worlds of experience."

Consistency and Credibility of the Brand World

The distinction of the Audi and Volkswagen brands is clearly visible on the dealer side. Dealers will invest $3.5 billion for this. Around the world, more than 11,000 Audi and Volkswagen businesses are undergoing refurbishing, and most of these were already redesigned by the end of 1999. These figures are an impressive illustration of the amount of confidence that our dealers have in the brands. The qualitative improvement in the dealer network is also reflected in the case of the Seat and Skoda brands, with the new corporate design and the new showroom designs.

Today, the customer expects a tailor-made range of mobility that goes far beyond the actual reputation of the automobile. This includes individual financing and leasing offers all the way to insurance services, telematics supplies, and telephone services. The Volkswagen marketing organization provides all of this in a manner consistent with the brand image.

However, customers also expect a sales and service mentality that meets their needs. As a result, we have developed a performance-oriented dealer margin system that includes customer satisfaction, as measured by market research, as one of the key components.

The customer orientation starts with the production of the vehicle. In the future, we therefore will be involving our customers in the actual production of their vehicles. The customers can, as it were, take part in the "birth" of their automobile. This is made possible in the new production facilities for the new deluxe models of the Volkswagen brand, the so-called "Gläserne Manufaktur" in Dresden. Customers can follow the creation of their motor car directly and personally.

Figure 4 shows that the climax of the stage setting for our brands is the Autostadt at Volkswagen headquarters in Wolfsburg.

An experience park is created around the automobile—with visions and attractions, with tomorrow's media and yesterday's memories—an unforgettable experience for every visitor. From June 2000, all visitors will

Figure 4   Autostadt.

have the opportunity to experience the world of the Volkswagen Group and each of its brands. Each brand has its own pavilion in which the corresponding "brand world" is staged in a fascinating way.

For those unable to visit Wolfsburg in person, an Internet program has been developed to provide an opportunity to experience the Autostadt virtually.

Today, it is very important for brands also to be positioned on the Internet. The automobile manufacturer's online activities on the Internet can be considered as a three-stage process. In the first phase, the provision of information remains the main objective. Volkswagen has been a pioneer in Europe with the first German home page by an automobile manufacturer. The second phase concentrates on creating an interactive dialog with customers. Here, Volkswagen not only began a dialog with customers via e-mail at an early date but also established chat groups for the Golf Generation in the context of the formation of online communities. In this case, the latest dialog platform is, for example, the Fan World, in which the hundreds of Volkswagen fan clubs throughout the world can exchange messages with each other. The Beetlemania Rally on the Internet also grabbed the attention of Internet users throughout the world who were asked to solve exciting tasks interactively together with the various teams that were on the road in Europe in the New Beetle. At the same time, the New Beetle was linked to the Internet online. The conspicuously painted New Beetles were later auctioned for good causes. In addition to the Internet, this event also attracted great attention in the press and television.

Finally, the third phase in the Internet activity deals with transactions and e-commerce. In the United States, 1 million vehicles are already being distributed via the Internet. For Europe, it is estimated that one day it will be possible to distribute 20 percent of all vehicles via the Internet.

Volkswagen therefore was one of the first motor car manufacturers to put what is known as a "Car Configurator" onto the Internet (Fig. 5), with which the customer can assemble his individual vehicle on screen. At the same time, the Configurator is linked directly to our Production Department's in-house model description system. This system, unlike the comparable ones, will configure only vehicles that can actually be constructed.

The vehicle request is then communicated to the dealer, describing what the customer has chosen from the dealer data base. The dealer will then make

Figure 5   Car Configurator.

the customer an individual offer and arrange for the experience of a test drive, which is a priority for a potential customer even in a virtual world.

4. Controlling the Multi-Brand Strategy

It is the task of marketing departments for the individual brands to use different marketing instruments to operationalize market missions and values. The efficiency and effectiveness of their measures are evaluated centrally. A brand control concept was developed to aid the management of the individual brands.

Brand management has three main functions:

- *Information*—Comparable data about the market placement of the different brands are provided regularly.

- *Planning*—The strategic and operative plans for the brands are coordinated during regular brand audits.

- *Control*—Target versus actual comparisons are the foundation of a directed management of the brands.

As an example, Fig. 6 presents the application of a method of brand controlling that is used to check brand awareness via target-actual comparisons. It
is called the semantic differential.

The semantic differential makes it possible to measure brand awareness based
on described attributes and associations. Pairs of opposites are used to present

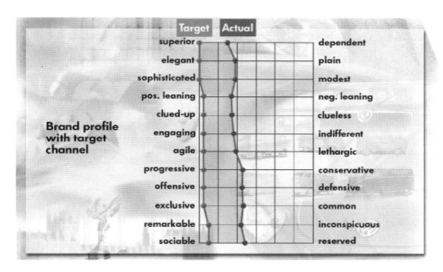

Figure 6 Semantic differential target channel (example).

the brand's "target profile" and compare it with the brand's "actual profile,"
which is derived from the definition of the brand personality. The result of this
comparison is the target channel. The goal is to minimize the delta in the
target channel through the use of corresponding marketing measures and to
establish the desired target awareness on the market or in the target group.

The measurement is conducted every two years for the major markets of all
brands. The results flow into the marketing plans for the brands and help to
steer brand policies.

These and other brand management tools provide precise conclusions about
the actual awareness of the brands on the market and their performance.

5. The Success of the Multi-Brand Strategy

The implementation of the brand personalities defined in the multi-brand strategy is a continuous process. The brand missions and the description of the exemplary images are target values that are implemented with the many different marketing instruments, so that the actual perception corresponds to the target perception.

The success of branding in the Volkswagen Group can best be documented by examining its market share. Between 1994 and 1999, the market share of the whole group in the five most important European markets increased from 15.8 to 18.9 percent (Fig. 7).

Loyalty across the whole group is approximately 10 percentage points above the average for the sector. At the same time, the rate of switching to Volkswagen has gone up by 25 percent. In absolute terms, this means an increase in the number of switches from other brands of 250,000 vehicles during the specified period.

These figures clearly demonstrate the success of rigorous branding in the multi-brand strategy and the significance of the development of strong brand personalities.

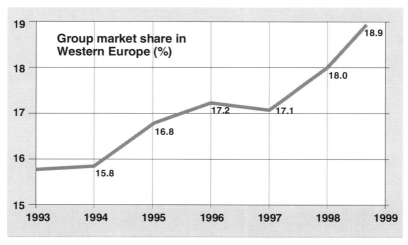

Figure 7   Increasing market share of the Volkswagen Group.

Connecting Your People with Your Brand, or The Magic of Practicing What You Preach

Ralf Landmann

> *Great brands are personal. They become an integral part of people's lives by forging emotional connections. We wanted to bring the brand to life... to express its specialness in people's lives.*
> —Deborah McCarthy, Coca-Cola

> *The next ten years will see a war among brands. It will be decided by a brand's image.*
> —J.J. Diaz Ruiz, Toyota

> *We are pushing to build brand awareness among Opel's employees.*
> —R. Hendry, CEO Opel

Practical insight on how to instill behavioral improvement with your employees, based on a hands-on approach to reaching your goals earlier, more easily, and more effectively.

Brands are among the most valuable assets of any company. From a consumer perspective, an orange is an orange—unless it's a Sunkist. From a business perspective, car manufacturers' brand values account for a substantial portion of their overall corporate value.

Enormous efforts are taken to introduce customers to distinct brand personalities. Cars, features, and qualities are less and less differentiating. Therefore, the values and attitudes of a given brand are carefully elaborated to help us, as customers, choose the "right" car and make. Based on these values, car makers not only promise but also hope for automotive dreamland: Loyal customers long for a lifetime relationship with a certain make and enthusiastically recommend their choice to others. Dealer franchise employees are consistently polite on the phone and exceed customer expectations regularly. They solve our car-insurance problems on the spot and are happy to explain competently what we did not understand on the company's website. Service- and salespeople work together in a process without flaws, and customers drive away with a positive image of the brand and its people—faithful to those who provided them with quality service...

Customers' physical experiences with you, your brand, and your retailers either build customer loyalty or inflict severe brand damage. Car manufacturers must ensure that they deliver what they promise and that they meet, indeed exceed, customer requirements. They must strengthen their brands and thus must convincingly align all three core areas of brand impact: products/services, employee behavior, and communication. The product itself and the respective market communication are only two ways to communicate and claim car brands' often proclaimed values such as commitment, innovation, intelligence, heritage, and perfection. Employee behavior is the third and vital one.

The frontline employees—the people in sales and service—have a tremendous impact on a brand's image and on the bottom line. With products of similar price, quality, features, design, and safety conditions, what can make all the difference is the quality of service that comes with the product. This realization has attracted managers more and more into the domain of the so-called "soft" disciplines, trying to align employee behavior with the brand image. Strategies and claims do not implement themselves, and processes cannot learn. People learn, and people drive processes.

This chapter focuses on how to connect frontline employees with the company's brand. It is generally about instilling behavioral change—where and how to begin, what to watch for, and how to set in motion a virtuous cycle to achieve and sustain behavioral improvement. It is based on Arthur D. Little's worldwide experience in brand, change, and knowledge management—within and beyond the automotive industry. What holds true for brand management also applies to many other corporate initiatives or occasions, for example:

- Post-merger integration
- e-business and mobile commerce
- Process improvement
- Cost reduction
- Innovation

Brands Are the Key to Survival

Factories make products, but customers buy brands. DaimlerChrysler's primary strength is neither its engineering nor its craftsmanship. It is the fact that people all around the globe dream of driving a Mercedes-Benz, put into conventional wisdom by Janis Joplin's famous song line, "Oh Lord, won't you buy me a Mercedes-Benz." This reflects DaimlerChrysler's growth and profit potential—planted in the heads of millions of potential buyers, making the Mercedes-Benz brand one of the most valuable in the (automotive) world. *Active* brand management has become a key issue. Products come and go, but successful brands will remain. Brands are and will be increasingly more important than factories, especially in a world that is rapidly moving from "brick and mortar" to "click and mortar." The war among automotive brands will be decided by brand images, posing three basic challenges:

- *Increasing difficulty to build and sustain real competitive advantage*—A little sportier, a little faster, a little more elegant, a bit roomier—not enough to distance yourself from the competition, to strengthen your brand, let alone gain the leading position

- *Increasing need for strong visions*—Car OEMs need a strong vision, a bold step forward to give new meaning to their brands, without endangering their heritage and tradition

- *Increasing need to teach, train, and coach employees*—Most employees have little or no idea of the brand, its importance, and their personal impact on it. How could they then possibly act in line with the brand?

The Challenge of Connecting Your People with Your Brand

"Connecting" simply means practicing what you preach. Behavior in line with the brand proves your claim and supports your image.

How disappointed are you if companies do not live up to their claims, not to speak of your real expectations? Connecting means putting your brand's values to life—by acting accordingly, every day, worldwide: in the showroom in New York, as well as in the repair shop in Buenos Aires, in sales and in service. The vice president of marketing in Tokyo and the service technician in Munich. To build and support a globally consistent image in line with the brand's values. Connecting should encompass all employees, but the focus should be on your frontline employees. Every employee is an integral part of your brand's specific service delivery chain, but frontline employees can make the difference. They are responsible for:

- Making a good first impression
- Anticipating, understanding, and fulfilling your customers' needs
- Reporting customers' feelings, comments, and attitudes to headquarters
- Helping management develop appropriate business plans

This type of relationship management—based on frontline employee behavior— separates your company from the competition. Establishing a vivid expression of your brand pays. Consider the example of AXA, one of the world's leading insurance companies, and its management style, as shown in Fig. 1.

Connecting your people with your brand, and the values for which it stands, produces bottom-line results, explaining automakers' and dealers' high investments in training their frontline employees to practice what is promised in the glittery world of advertising (and is well remembered by customers).

Connecting is far from easy. Most employees have seen so many customer care, total quality, and excellence programs come and go. The rationale, objectives, and progress of those programs often remained unclear, worsened by the fact that frontline employees usually are among a company's most critical groups (Fig. 2).

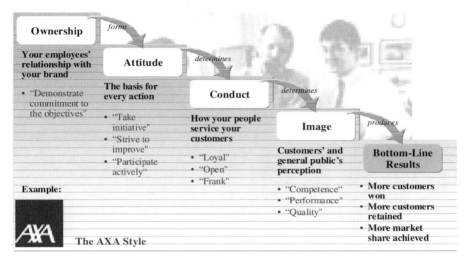

Source: www.axa.com, added with comments from the author

Figure 1   Establishing a vivid expression of your brand pays.

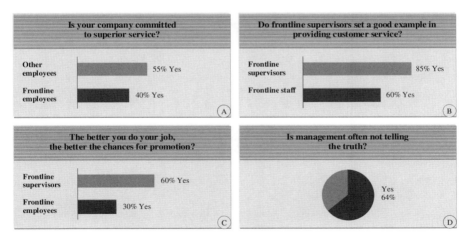

Sources: A, B, C-Abt. Associates 1995; D: Council of Communication Management, 1994

*Figure 2   Selected survey results illustrate frontline employees'
perception compared to other employee groups.*

A Practical Approach to Achieve and Sustain Behavioral Improvement

To effectively instill brand-suitable behavioral change within a global organization, consider companies with the scope and size of General Motors, Ford, Toyota, Volkswagen, Renault/Nissan, or DaimlerChrysler. Employees worldwide must be integrated into both the development and the rollout of any such program. They should hear about the brand vision and values and why the brand is personally important for them. They should understand their personal impact on the brand in order to act in line with it. As an ideal result, the brand values and their implications for day-to-day customer interactions have found their way into the

- Heads (understanding)
- Hearts (feeling)
- Hands (doing)

of employees worldwide—in different countries, from diverse cultural backgrounds, and different functions and hierarchies. Most companies, and especially car OEMs, have collected wide experience regarding how to initiate, support, and sustain change initiatives. Several critical success factors for sustainable improvement are (theoretically) observed, as shown in Fig. 3.

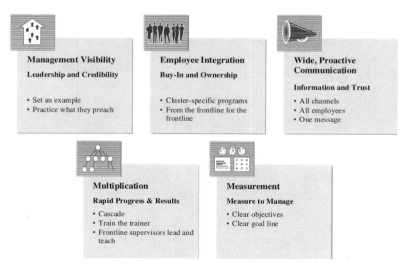

Figure 3 Critical success factors for sustainable improvement.

130

However, this is easier said than done. When attempting to implement a program to improve behavior in line with the brand, past experiences warn us of the typical vicious circle of so many internal change initiatives, regardless of what they were attempting to do. Management starts a new program where employee behavior and involvement are crucial. After a grand kickoff, employees' attitudes and performance initially do respond to management's pressure with an apparent positive peak. However, after a while, everything returns to the same level at which it started. The program is considered to be flawed, and another initiative is launched. Again and again, people are called to actively participate, as cynicism and resistance increase. Change fatigue emerges, and behavioral improvement is farther away than ever.

Building a Solid Platform for Behavioral Improvement

A solid platform for a successful change program rests on three pillars:

- Observing past experiences with change-initiatives: What works, and what does not?

- Defining a consistent message: What do we want to communicate?

- Clustering your target audience: Who do we want to reach? And how?

Any successful change program requires deep insight into the past experience with change initiatives within the company. Start by conducting interviews with key people at all levels, functions, and regions of the company, and ask them two basic questions: (1) How was the last program? and (2) What do we need to observe?

As a rule of thumb for large-scale organizations, for every 1,000 employees at least one such in-depth interview should be conducted, with the minimum number being 30. Not only do these interviews provide you with priceless input on "Do's" and "Don't's" but they also provide the basis to design a program that could produce the right flow from "head" through "heart" to "hands." Good interviews, conducted with external support, allow the units' ideas, requirements, and experiences to be incorporated into the program and help to identify the company- and unit-specific key success factors. Typical interview feedback on behavioral change initiatives within the automotive industry includes statements such as:

- "As long as management does not change, neither will the employees." (Sales executive, Germany)

- "Tangible content in an easy way, but please not another program." (After-market executive, Brazil)

- "Build up emotion and excitement, but not another 'hooray' event." (Marketing manager, France)

- "There has to be a credible, convincing process owner, with access to the right people." (Project manager, Germany)

- "Integration of dealers is crucial, as they drive client satisfaction." (Market manager, Italy)

The second important pillar of any change or improvement program is a clear and concise message. Three work streams must be tackled: (1) a *clear* measurable definition of general value statements, (2) convincing answers for seven critical questions, and (3) a thought-through core script[1] for top-down communication.

Consider typical automotive value propositions randomly taken from current business magazines:

- "A car that follows your heart wherever it goes" (Audi)
- "We try harder" (Avis)
- "The relentless pursuit of perfection" (Lexus)
- "Live a little every day" (Toyota)
- "People finding a better way" (Dana)

How do these propositions translate into actual behavior? "The relentless pursuit of perfection"—what exactly does it mean to the Lexus salesperson? How should she or he behave in a specific situation? What are the service technicians supposed to do differently to relentlessly pursue perfection? Do

---

1 What we refer to as "core script" is a slightly altered approach based on Noel Tichy's so-called "Teachable Point of View," in Suzy Wetlaufer's "Driving Change—An Interview with Ford Motor Company's Jacques Nasser," *Harvard Business Review*, March–April 1999, pp. 77–88.

they have the means to do so? How will they be measured? How do they know they have crossed the goal line? How is this message perceived and understood in different cultures? Is it accepted? These and other questions demand convincing answers. Marketing must explain its brand positioning and value proposition to the frontline sales- and service-people. In turn, they need to transfer this model into (new) tangible behavioral patterns—in line with the brand's positioning.

Experience shows that a clear and concise message is most effectively elaborated when prepared centrally at the top and then actively discussed and refined with the target groups' direct supervisors. The core message itself is not open for discussion, whereas areas of local adaptation and the pathway to achieve the desired behavioral improvement in that particular division must be. A true involvement of local management—as opposed to one centrally developed message and program for all units, markets, and regions—produces better programs.

When elaborating the core message of a program, seven critical questions demand convincing and well-thought-through answers to inspire people to follow:

1. *Why is this change urgent?* What is driving us? Why might this effort actually matter?

2. *Who wants it to happen?* Who has set our program as a priority? Are there clearly defined sponsors? What might be the reasoning behind their request?

3. *What results do we want to produce?* What, specifically, is the change we are seeking? If the change takes place, what will that obtain for us? How will our efforts benefit our customers?

4. *How will we change?* What kinds of new capabilities will we need to develop? How will we develop them? Which aspects of our current work and practices will be affected by the change? What challenges do we expect to face? How could we prepare for them?

5. *Who will be involved, and where is our support?* Will the initiative mean new activities for everyone? Should other people be included?

6. *What do I, personally, have to do?* When will our initiative begin? What steps do I need to take, and in which domain? What do I hope to learn? What skills and capabilities would I like to gain? What do we want to do first?

7. *What's in it for me?* If I change, what is my personal benefit?

Invest in properly addressing these basic issues. Answer the questions sufficiently in a one-day workshop with top management. Do not prepare an impressive presentation, but instead develop a handwritten, short, and simple reasoning in the CEO's own words—the core script. Then, as indicated here, refine the script, take new ideas aboard, and test it with selected colleagues and representatives of the target group—without questioning it as a whole. Incorporate their feedback as feasible. This (authentic and tested) core script not only provides the guidelines for the program but also anticipates the answers to employees' concerns.

The third important pillar of any change or improvement program is a clear picture of whom and how you want to reach with your program to instill behavioral improvement in line with the brand. Figure 4 provides an overview of criteria to segment your internal target audience. To effectively reach a service technician in Buenos Aires and a marketing executive in New York, very different methods and channels of knowledge transfer and communication will have to be used.

Segmentation of your target audience often takes longer than expected, mostly because the relevant data are not readily available, even in companies with sophisticated HR systems. We estimate a three-month effort to gather the data previously mentioned for a division employing approximately 100,000 employees. In one case, as a positive side effect of such an exercise, 1,600 employees were identified who for years had received CD-ROMs for distance-learning purposes but did not even have access to a PC with a CD-drive. Segmentation means to identify human beings and their experience behind anonymous headcount figures.

After you have built your solid program platform (taking into account past experiences with change initiatives in your company), developed the core script, and clustered your target audience, it is time to finalize your program and execute it.

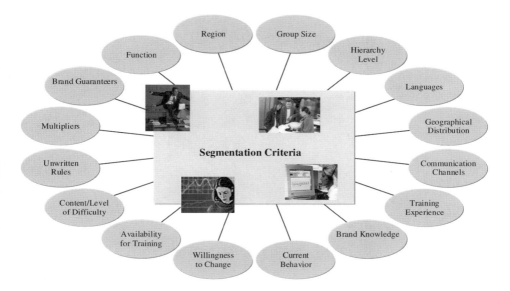

Figure 4. Identify whom you want to reach and how you want to reach them—by analyzing and clustering your target audience along recommended segmentation criteria.

Successful Program Execution

When finalizing your program, three key success factors reappear in any initiative to instill behavioral improvement: (1) the need to address two axes—knowledge and behavior; (2) the need to align the company's and the individual's objectives; and (3) the need to incorporate proven guiding principles of successful change initiatives.

To effectively instill behavioral improvement, both knowledge and behavior must be addressed in parallel (Fig. 5).

The more people know about their jobs, the better they are able to perform ("head" and "hands"). Thus, the knowledge/cognitive component must be addressed. In parallel, the emotional/affective component must be satisfied to develop ownership for the brand and to act accordingly—every day, worldwide, on the basis of emotional involvement ("heart"). This in turn requires,

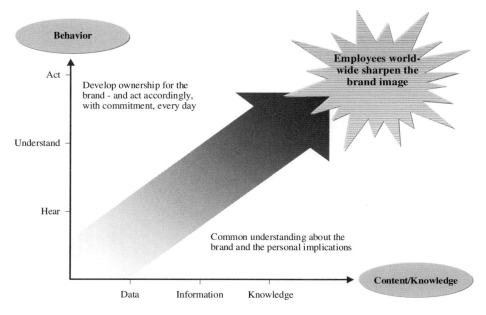

Figure 5   Address two dimensions—knowledge and behavior.

among other criteria, the alignment of individual and company objectives. Any program opposing an individual's values and beliefs, holding him or her back from attaining personal objectives, has very low chances of gaining support and is doomed to fail. Program initiators must know what makes their employees come to work on Monday morning.

Individual motivators in the work force of a given company are amazingly similar due to the existence of strong organizational cultures that select and shape behavior. Individuals who do not share the same values and beliefs normally are rejected by the system, and they either isolate themselves within the company or leave. An analysis of the unwritten rules of more than 100 companies all over the world has shown us that a maximum of six motivators are always present in one or another combination in most companies today:

- To perform a meaningful or challenging job
- To learn from the job or the colleagues
- To work in a friendly atmosphere

- To belong to a world-class company
- To influence the direction of the company
- To be recognized by the customers or colleagues for contributions

A seventh motivator—job security—appeared only in situations of deep crisis and soon was replaced by others when the crisis ended.

After you have formulated your ideas about how to address the two axes and how to align individual and company objectives, you should step back and reconsider general guiding principles for any change initiative, proven in companies around the world. On that basis, you must finalize your initiative to become both company and culture specific (Fig. 6).

Apart from these general principles to instill behavioral improvement, communication in the widest sense of the word plays the key role in building and sustaining the process to improve behavior in line with the brand. Bear in mind that:

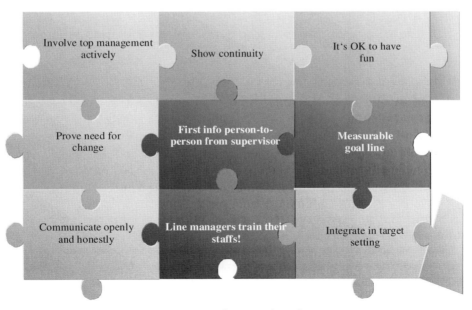

Figure 6 Key success factors for change initiatives.

- No amount of communication can change deeply held beliefs and values.

- The more people have the feeling of being well informed, the more likely they will agree with a program.[2]

- Movies, videos, and publications are useful supportive tools, but not for introducing behavioral improvement to frontline employees.[3]

- Face-to-face communication is the most effective means to change behavior.

- The first words frontline employees hear about a change should come from the person to whom they are closest: their supervisor.

- To achieve behavioral improvement, major content input should come from the participants themselves.

- The only way to really communicate a desired way of behavior is to act in accordance with it ("try harder") and to give others the incentive to do the same.

- To motivate employees, communicate relative performance (this group in relation to...).

Only the perfect, company-specific combination of heads, hearts, and hands can produce the collective miracle. A program for behavioral improvement in line with the brand requires a unique combination of knowledge, emotion, and support in implementation. These cannot be reproduced in other companies; each case is specific. Most important is the distinction "in that company" or "in that community," because change and communication on change are driven locally. Knowing the motivators of the work force, it will not be difficult to

---

2 This insight should affect the frequency, rate of redundancy, and directness of communication ("straight talk").

3 British employees rate videos 13th out of 16 ways to receive information. Seventy-five percent of companies that have used videos believe they are ineffective. Publications are rated by employees as untrustworthy and often incomprehensible. In T.J. Larkin and Sandar Larkin's "Reaching and Changing Frontline Employees," *Harvard Business Review*, May–June 1996, New York, pp. 95–104.

see how they relate to the company objectives. It then will be easier to see if you have selected the right incentives and whether you are calling on the work force with the right message.

In large organizations—for instance, the sales and service operations of any global car OEM—executives face the challenge of having to deliver a global program while also acknowledging the importance of cultural differences and the diversity of professional roles and responsibilities. Culture, as a shared way of assigning meaning and as a national set of values, beliefs, habits, customs, and norms, has a tremendous impact on organizational behavior. Ford in Cologne, Germany, is very different from Ford in Sharonville, Ohio. Rover in Longbridge, U.K., is very different from BMW in Spartanburg, South Carolina, distinguished by its own written and unwritten rules that are clearly understand-able only to those working there. The specific organizational cultures influence how the company or division operates and how people interact with each other and the outside world. A sales operation in Japan probably has a very different pattern in solving problems than a truck plant in the outskirts of São Paulo, Brazil. This diversity makes it so difficult to successfully plan and implement programs to instill behavioral improvement in line with the brand. "Commit-ment," "going the extra mile," and other popular claims in the world of brand positioning have very different meanings within the same company across dif-ferent divisions, functions, countries, age groups, etc. Emotions are aroused by different standards in different cultures; therefore, deep knowledge about the local reality is extremely important in any behavioral improvement program. You must identify the key variations of cultural diversity in order to effectively develop and implement your program:

- *Leadership style and role assumption*—Leading, recognizing efforts, communicating, and motivating employees is culturally bound. Power, achievement, and the degree in which roles are embedded in the lives of the individuals are strongly influenced by their culture.

- *The decision-making process*—The way decisions are made, conflict is resolved, risk is perceived, and negotiations are carried out and closed.

- *The way people interact in teams*—How they define the task, carry out the work, and deliver the results is a function of ascription or achievement.

- *The way people learn*—Individual versus group skills development are highly dependent on cultural patterns. Training methods, tools, and methodologies are culturally colored.

- *The way people communicate*—Their language abilities, the style of communication, the rules and social competencies required are all defined by culture.

From our experience, we recommend spending a maximum of 60–70 percent of the effort in the development of a behavioral improvement initiative *centrally*. This leaves enough time and resources for *local* adaptation for knowledge transfer and communication. This approach ensures both global direction and local interpretation, rather than a "one-size-fits-all" approach, which can jeopardize the acceptance and success of a global initiative.

Rollout

With preparation of your initiative as outlined here, you have laid the essential groundwork to roll out a successful program. Again, experience with large organizations in general, and global operating car OEMs in particular, indicates four key success factors that depend directly on the preparatory work in advance:

1. Have the direct supervisor provide the first information about a new initiative.

2. Make line managers train their staffs.

3. Provide support with an integrated training and communication program.

4. Have a measurable goal line.

The first information about a new initiative must come from the direct supervisor. That rule must apply to all hierarchy levels of an organization. Starting at the very top, the core script is delivered top down in personal, one-to-one, face-to-face meetings with their respective direct reports. The core script—as previously outlined here—explains the rationale for the program: Why are we doing this? What do we expect? What is your commitment (goal line)? The tone is open, honest, and direct, not a rehearsed announcement in a conference center or in the global business TV. It is simply a person-to-person, fact-driven conversation, enabling a fast, personal multiplication of the core message of the initiative.

Just as important as the personal multiplication by the supervisors is the principle that line managers train their staffs themselves. Instilling behavioral improvement is not something to fully delegate to trainers outside the line of command. The necessary momentum for change is created if line managers step up in front of their direct reports and

- Explain that they are conducting the training themselves because it is such an important issue

- Prove that they are measured on the success of their efforts and that they in turn will measure their direct reports on how well they live up to expectations and deliver the message in turn

After line managers have trained their direct reports personally, they must act in accordance with what they taught. They have no choice but to actually practice what they preach—by "trying harder" or "relentlessly pursuing perfection."

Both the person-to-person delivery of the core script and the line managers' active training role must be supported by a company-specific portfolio of proven training/coaching and communication modules, as identified in the platform-building phase (interviews). Experience from numerous assignments we have performed indicates that people in the Western world tend to prefer emotional appeal (theater/cinema) over classic classroom settings. Thus, programs often incorporate group activities with a high emotional component to build up and sustain commitment—on a sufficiently cognitive basis to prevent the slightest notion of "phoniness." Complementary communication modules help to create awareness and support participants in understanding and accepting the core message of the program, sustaining the process and leading to measurable results.

Measurable results are essential in monitoring the overall success of your program and even more in motivating its participants. As Lawrence Bossidy puts it, "People must believe they can win. You have to define a goal line, so if they're successful, they have a chance to stop and say 'Hey, this is a victory.' Celebration is crucial." In that respect, two elements help to both monitor and motivate throughout the program: (1) applying a program-specific balanced scorecard, and (2) the integration of the program objectives into the individual target-setting, performance, and appraisal processes.

We have covered the major steps and key success factors to plan and roll out a large-scale initiative to improve behavior in line with the brand. In essence, it is based on solid preparation, open and fact-driven dialog, a top-down communication flow, and active involvement by all line managers to train their staffs themselves. This approach is proven, especially within the automotive industry. A number of OEMs successfully apply it, with their company-specific adaptations. Behind this approach is a deep commitment to six guiding principles to build and sustain trust (Fig. 7).

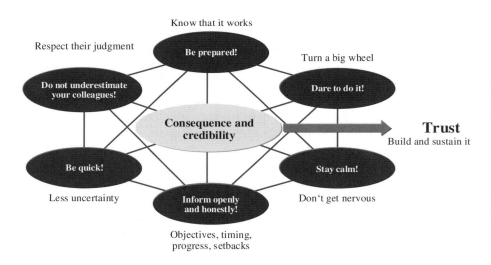

Figure 7   Six guiding principles to build and sustain trust.

As an automotive executive—preferably in marketing or brand management—you should consider these six questions:

- What is your brand's claim?

- How many people should live up to that claim daily, worldwide? Do they?

- How many moments of truth in direct customer contact take place daily?

- Do your (frontline) employees know examples of how to behave in line with your brand?

- Do they know how to act in edge situations?

- Does your reward system support brand-suitable behavior?

You could unleash the potential of your brand by training, teaching, and coaching your employees on your brand's values—to connect them with your brand, to practice what you preach, and to provide service, in the same way as Henry Ford did. He claimed that the Model T was so durable and simple to service that if one could not be fixed, he would replace it for free. A farmer from Michigan wrote him a letter, telling him that no one was able to repair his "Tin Lizzy." Two weeks later, a very surprised farmer received a new Model T.

Literature

Best of the Best Colloquium—An Exchange of Knowledge Among Leading Practitioners in Customer Management, Arthur D. Little, 1995.

Karmasin, Helene, *Produkte als Botschaften*, Wirtschaftsverlag Carl Ueberreuter, Vienna, Austria, 1998.

Larkin, T.J., and Larkin, Sandar, "Reaching and Changing Frontline Employees," *Harvard Business Review*, May–June 1996, New York, NY, pp. 95–104.

Maira, Arun, and Scott-Morgan, Peter, *The Accelerating Organization—Embracing the Human Face of Change*, McGraw-Hill, New York, NY, 1997.

Pfeiffer, Jeffrey, *The Human Equation—Building Profits by Putting People First*, Harvard Business School Press, Boston, MA, 1998.

Rosenfeld, Jill, "Experience the Real Thing—The Coca-Cola Branding Experience in Las Vegas," *Fast Company*, January/February 2000, p. 184.

Wetlaufer, Suzy, "Driving Change—An Interview with Ford Motor Company's Jacques Nasser," *Harvard Business Review*, March–April 1999, pp. 77–88.

The author would like to thank Claudia Bock-Valotta for her valuable contributions.

Automotive Industry: Automotive Giants Get Ready for the e-Business Age!

Jochen Funk

The automotive industry today ranks among the most established and mature industries of the Western world. Recent consolidation will only further the well-established dominance of the big corporations. It is a global industry. Parts production, system and module composition, and car assembly take place virtually all over the world before a car is sold off the dealer's lot.

The automobile has not lost any of its original fascination for consumers world-wide. Some classic models have become so firmly entrenched in the affection of buyers that some car makers have even turned out revamped editions. Is there anyone who really hates the Volkswagen Beetle?

Car makers have pioneered management and manufacturing concepts such as lean production, simultaneous engineering, and Japanese *Kaizen*. The sophistication of production methods at every level of supplier and manufacturing quality at assembly plants has risen to impressive heights.

However, evolution rather than revolution characterizes the industry as a whole: Engineering and products are the main engines of innovation. Response to changing consumer habits and preferences is slow, and new product development is lengthy. It is not unusual for new models to hit the streets after four to seven years on the drawing boards.

The future is not all rosy. Sales and service traditionally compose a network of medium-sized car dealers that know how to push the product on the market. The current overproduction in the car industry, however, should make a transition to market-pull strategies mandatory. This will prove challenging, because cars are so much alike in design, features, and technological quality that manufacturers are relying increasingly on branding to achieve their desired positioning.

Now witness a new type of industry. It comprises companies often in existence no longer than five years. They are flexible and lean, make decisions in the flash of an eye, promote entrepreneurship at every level of the organization, and rarely view a challenge as something impossible to meet. These are the pioneering enterprises of the e-business age. They have turned, almost overnight, into service providers with global presence. Their extraordinarily rapid ascent has led to a stock market capitalization that enables them to raise equity funds rivaling the capacity of well-established industries.

Naturally, the automotive industry has eyed these developments with great interest. Companies such as autobytel.com or Microsoft's CarPoint are poised to appropriate the position that until now was held firmly by traditional car dealers. When this takes hold, it will alter irrevocably relationships throughout the automotive value chain. It is not surprising that Mark Hogan, former vice president of General Motors' small-cars operation and current head of General Motors' new e-Business Division, states, "We've come to realize that if we don't move with Internet speed, we could become extinct."

Although car makers may not be the champions of fast change, the promise of e-business—and the companies that have recognized and exploited it—has set even the biggest car makers in motion. This chapter provides an overview of the innovations the industry has implemented thus far and will need to implement in response to the rise of e-business, and it illustrates how these innovations change the automotive value chain. We will examine how car manufacturers are organizing and deriving maximum benefit from e-business.

Four Levels of Innovation

For car manufacturers to reach online customers, they must innovate in marketing. Manufacturers and independent parties initially created Web pages using multiple-choice options and 3-D virtual showroom technologies that enabled potential car buyers to configure their cars before entering the physical showroom. At the same time, manufacturers used advanced data mining techniques to identify which customer type is interested in which equipment features of the car.

The second step in innovation is provided by the aforementioned online referral services for dealers, such as autoweb.com and autobytel.com, and by transaction-oriented "car brokers," of which carsdirect.com and carorder.com are examples. These innovative e-business models threaten to relegate traditional dealerships to mere pickup points for car buyers. Online car dealerships are already buying traditional dealerships to ensure supply from manufacturers, while retail chains in the United Kingdom are starting to invest in ramp-up centers for serving online dealerships with cars.

In the third step of the innovation process, manufacturers have set up their own online services, such as GM BuyPower. Planning and production can be optimized so that a new product can evolve: Web cars, specifically manufactured to be sold over the World Wide Web. This development could conceivably branch off in a totally new direction, such as an Internet-equipped and information technology-stuffed vehicle—the PC on wheels.

Finally, the sector arrives at the fourth level of innovation, where the entire business model can shift. Car manufacturers transform from product manufacturers to integrated service providers. The vehicle remains at the core of the offering, but it is surrounded by additional services such as mobility concepts, which are independent of any particular vehicle. Wireless Internet access will accelerate this trend, when the UMTS standard will be introduced in 2003 as the successor of GSM in most European countries. Customers may be offered a combination of services for which they are charged monthly fees.

Looking past the fourth innovation level, car manufacturers may harvest sufficient fees from the referral or linking of clients to advertising, tourism, petrochemicals, and telecommunications companies that, in the end, the buyer's monthly leasing account is sufficiently credited for him to ride his new car for free.

Impact on the Value Chain

Obviously, such innovations as discussed here cannot but change the value chain. e-business provides the efficient and timesaving tools to speed

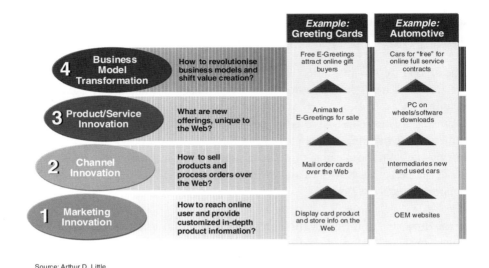

Source: Arthur D. Little

Figure 1   Four levels of e-business innovation.

information from consumers to manufacturers and suppliers. At every interface in the value chain, this will bring about changes. What will the new order-to-delivery cycle look like?

The business-to-consumer interface is improved through the marketing innovations of car configurators or one-stop-shopping opportunities that include financing, insurance, and extended warranty. The business-to-business interfaces between the manufacturer and first-tier suppliers of modules or systems, as well as suppliers on the following tiers, are organized through electronic marketplaces. Two mutually connected extranets will reduce coordination and modification costs and realize the targeted order-to-delivery time span (Fig. 2).

It is expected that the diminishing group of mega-suppliers with sales volumes exceeding 10 billion U.S. dollars will take over greater parts of car production, such as complete car interiors or electronics and safety systems. In keeping with this change, manufacturers will focus their core manufacturing competencies on the car body and engine. Their main roles will be concept, design, and assembly on the one hand, and branding and marketing on the other. Manufacturers will be integrators of both front and back ends.

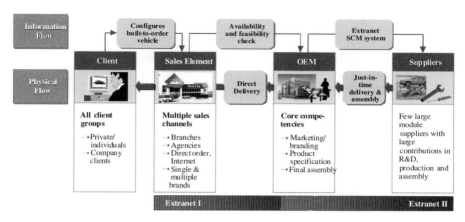

Source: Arthur D. Little

Figure 2 Built-to-order vehicles will be ready for pickup within a few days.

Even where car manufacturers cling to their current indirect sales channel strategies, better-informed customers will affect the traditional dealer's role. Perfect market transparency, so far one of the major obstacles for European consumers, will shift bargaining power to the demand side. Economies of scale will drive small- and medium-sized car dealers into large dealer combinations at the risk of becoming obsolete. An alternative may be to become service centers, which are not limited to car repair and inspection services.

At the same time, some manufacturers may take advantage of new legislative possibilities and set up direct sales channels themselves. Standard car models can be sold at discount rates. Independent multi-brand agencies can act as price brokers, managing the best deal for consumers.

New passenger-car market entrants might seize the opportunity to use Internet intermediaries to market their cars. Remaining dealer functions such as pickup and service could be organized through external services, thus limiting the so-far considerable market entry barriers.

The Mobile Twist

The Internet and advancing technologies in mobile data communication have added another twist to the car manufacturer's perception of his business and the value of his customers. Billions of wasted dashboard eyeball-hours every year are the new prime target for companies seeking to deliver their content and commerce offerings to consumers while on the move. Whereas the first Internet wave is in full thrust to take the car into the Web, it is being overtaken by a second one, taking the Web into the car.

A variety of applications will be seen in cars, where Internet access will be the underlying technology, even if the driver will not notice. These will range from safety features such as automatic emergency calls and onboard diagnostics, over travel-related location-based services and interactive "infotainment" offerings, to business productivity services, where tasks so far reserved to a work space can be transferred into your car. The underlying technologies are already on their way to market.

The fast technological evolution yields tremendous opportunities for car manufacturers to build closer relationships with their customers. To do so, they will have to be a vital part of the portal the users will access while being in their cars. Will it be car manufacturers selling advertising space on their dashboards, or will it be car manufacturers having to pay for obtaining access to their own cars and their own customers? To ensure that revenues are flowing in the right direction, car manufacturers will have to act quickly and signal the market that the dashboards in their cars are already occupied by a solution they have created.

Preparing the Organization

The daunting question for any multibillion-dollar car manufacturer must be how to prepare the organization for the age of e-business. The industry's characteristic lack of flexibility makes implementing the fast decision-making processes needed for e-business difficult. The trial-and-error approaches that are customary among successful e-business startups are in stark contrast to the long-term strategic planning to which car makers are accustomed.

The apparent answer is not to build the e-business from within, but from outside, the organization. An exception is General Motors, which set up a separate e-GM unit with approximately 300 staff. For established manufacturers that opt to create new and independent ventures, partnerships and joint ventures seem to be prerequisite in the customer-focused environment of e-business. These companies bring in the knowledge required to take advantage of real-time consumer preferences, by mastering the data mining requirements and the integration of different system architectures. Their core business is not manufacturing and retailing automobiles but to provide a wide range of different services. The product-oriented car manufacturers will be able to achieve this transition with the help of information technology specialists. Joint ventures such as the Ford cooperation with Microsoft's MSN CarPoint on the retail side and with Oracle on the supply side so far are the most remarkable moves in this direction.

Those companies that become stuck in internal politics and develop risk-minimization strategies will miss the train entirely. Therefore, car manufacturers are being forced to form flexible decision-making structures as quickly as possible, for example:

- Cooperation GM with AOL Time Warner
- Cooperation Ford with Yahoo!

The car in the Internet and the Internet in the car: e-commerce is converging with telematics in a broad sense.

Deriving Maximum Benefits from e-Business

The challenges the automotive industry faces with regard to the e-business age are enormous. Nevertheless, adequate moves have been made in the right directions even before the e-business hype started. No matter what media the consumers will use to buy automotive products and services, they will settle with reliable brands while searching through the jungle of offerings. They will most appreciate the integrated services of an aligned organization, and it will be an exciting while efficient shopping experience based on superb customer management. All these factors make customers cling to the companies with which they have already dealt.

Therefore, the three key questions car manufacturers must answer to derive maximum benefits from e-business are:

- How should we position our brand(s) on the Web?

- How can we ensure a mutually useful customer relationship, enabling us to build lifelong customer retention?

- How can we ensure that the organization will continually adapt to the accelerating changes in the environment?

Perhaps above all, management and employees of car manufacturers, as well as their suppliers, must change their mindsets. At the end of the day, an automotive industry in the traditional sense will not exist. Rather, automotive-related activities will converge in an e-business community.

Although perhaps offering no solace for car manufacturers in the short run, the by-now famous remark of General Electric CEO Jack Welsh, Jr., serves as a clear reminder that doing nothing in the age of e-business will get you nowhere:

> Where does the Internet rank in priority? It's number 1, 2, 3, and 4.

Improving Processes and Exploiting Potential for Optimization— But How?

Heiko Wolters, Jochen Funk

> *If the only tool you have is a hammer,*
> *then every problem looks like a nail.*
> —Abraham Maslow

The increasing level of competition in the last few years has significantly increased the demands made on automobile companies. To ensure rapid development times, low costs, high quality, and a consistent orientation toward the customer, the old structures must be rethought and a process-oriented philosophy must be introduced in the companies. Re-engineering measures often do not go far enough because they merely focus on processes and neglect associated areas such as information technology, organization, or culture and behavior.

In addition, the benefits of the optimization of the business processes can be fully realized only if changes are successfully implemented—change management thus receives critical importance. This means initiating on the employee level a change of consciousness. On the other hand, on the organizational level, it means building change agents and making the transition from a project-management to a process-oriented company organization structure. Only a well-managed implementation ensures the success of the initiative.

From the Functional to the Process-Oriented Organization

The traditional automobile markets are displaying signs of saturation, globalization has considerably increased competition, and the demands of customers have increased continually. Automotive companies can no longer differentiate themselves using high-quality products. Instead, they must guarantee low prices, rapid delivery times, and excellent service. Although these challenges are not new in principle, many companies are having trouble meeting these requirements because their structures and processes are not sufficiently oriented toward the customer.

In the past, companies could achieve significant economies of scale through functional specialization with a homogenous product program and by being successfully active in the marketplace. In contrast, in today's complex and dynamic environment in which integrated solutions and a rapid time-to-market are required, many more departments must cooperate and be oriented toward the customer. A lack of alignment among departments, interface problems, or even divisional egotism unavoidably leads to nonfulfillment of the factors for success demanded by the market. For example, if Purchasing wishes to select a supplier, it might find out that Development is already working with companies that are innovative but do not meet the price and quality demands of the marketplace. The consequence of this inadequate coordination among departments is products that are too expensive and lack the necessary quality, as well as delays in approval of suppliers.

The classic, functional orientation that is still found in many companies therefore must give way to a process-oriented organization that understands customer-orientation thoroughly as the basis for its actions (Fig. 1). Coherent processes and responsibility structures, therefore, are a requirement for the coordinated cooperation of the various departments in a company. Accordingly, such an organization is ideally structured horizontally by processes under the responsibility of process owners rather than vertically by function.

The advantages associated with a consistent process orientation of the company are numerous: The processes become leaner and require fewer resources. The connections among the individual organizational units increase flexibility, raise quality, and reduce throughput times. The customer profits from these efforts.

However, in the last few years, many companies have attempted to create such a process-oriented philosophy, with little success. A study conducted by

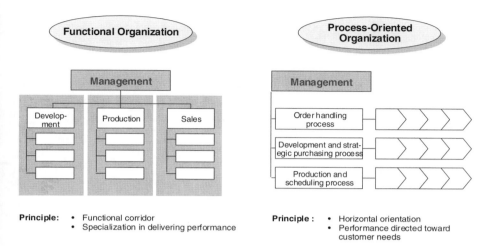

Figure 1   Functional versus process-oriented organization.

Arthur D. Little on the topic of organizational change showed that 66 percent of those questioned were dissatisfied with the results of process re-engineering projects. Two difficulties were listed frequently in this context by the companies: (1) to define, optimize, and document the important processes and interfaces, and (2) to initiate change in the company and to maintain implementation of the processes in the long run. Both topics are discussed in the following.

Introduction of a Process-Oriented Company Philosophy

Although the processes should remain the focus during the introduction of a process-oriented company philosophy, additional considerations are required to achieve a long-lasting optimization of the firm. These include impact on the company organizational structure, the IT environment, the company culture, and employee behavior. Often, the different areas influence each other. For example, processes cannot survive when the company organizational structures do not support them. Only when all four of the adjustment levers mentioned here are in alignment can any long-lasting process optimization be successfully implemented (Fig. 2).

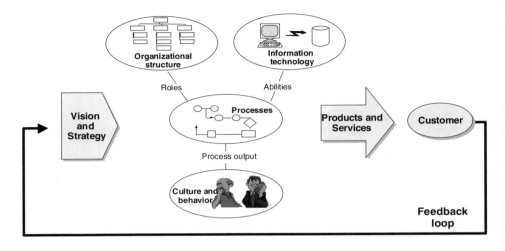

Figure 2 The four adjustment levers of process optimization.

The process analysis, the core of the efforts for improvement, is performed in four steps. The first phase deals with determining how much process analysis is necessary. The second phase focuses on the actual mapping and analysis of the processes selected. The actual process optimization is done in the third phase, followed by the implementation of the new processes in the fourth phase.

Determining the Critical Business Processes and the Extent of the Process Analysis

For reasons of complexity, it makes little sense to tackle every process in a company for optimization at the same time. Instead, the critical business processes must be identified so that the available resources can be usefully targeted and employed while not burdening the daily business. The critical business processes can be recognized because (1) they often cover several functions or even organizations, (2) they are perceptible to external suppliers and customers, (3) they have an influence on stakeholder interests, and (4) they exhibit a high degree of linked activities. Beyond that, they are generally characterized by high resource requirements. These critical business processes are different from company to company, as well as from industry to industry. Although a supplier of commodity parts, for example, sees very inexpensive production as critical for his business, the supplier of complex systems sees the processes that deal with system management, development and logistics, and their alignment as crucial for success.

The level of process improvement that is necessary depends on the intensity with which improvements have been carried out in the past in the company and the goals being pursued. While "incremental improvements" aim to make only minor improvements in existing processes, redesign is directed at more extensive improvements. This includes, for example, the redefinition of processes and the interfaces affected. A rethink occurs when new processes that did not previously exist are introduced (Fig. 3).

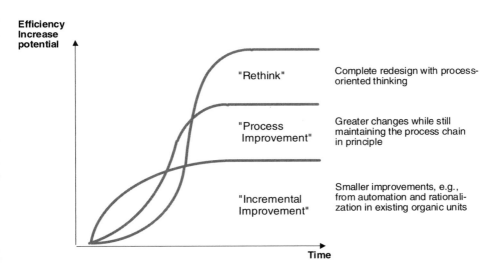

Figure 3   Rethink versus redesign versus incremental improvement.

Mapping the Processes

In this phase, the processes affected are analyzed and documented. In addition, the responsibilities within the process are defined.

Before the start of the process analysis, decisions must be made on the use of suitable software to support the analysis and documentation of the processes.

This decision should depend on the company-specific requirements and the future use of the documented process. If the processes are recorded only for certification purposes, a graphically oriented software package is normally adequate. For extensive calculation, analysis software is necessary. Accordingly, the tools vary from those only for process display all the way to complex software with an extensive reference database which makes possible pure process modeling and simulation. The selection of the tools also determines the form of display of the process and the syntax employed. The use of event-controlled process chains as display form has become largely standard, based on its closeness to the widespread enterprise system SAP.

A common understanding of the process is essential for the accuracy of the process recorded—especially when several organizational units are affected by the analysis. Typically, a process can be defined as a series of logically connected actions that lead to a specific result. Processes can transcend both functions and companies. Added value, in the classical way, is not always an element in a process, as supportive functions may dominate.

The extent and breadth of the processes occurring in the companies often are not even transparent for the actual users. The users, depending on their viewpoint, hold different interpretations of the contents of the process. Multi-departmental brainstorming and a Delphi analysis are effective methods that can be used to quickly gain an overview of the processes under examination. Eventually, the processes must be accurately defined with regard to contents and goals.

Depending on the number of activities, the mapping of the process and its analysis can be quite a complex procedure. To provide an overview, the processes should first be grouped by subject. Examples of possible groupings are value added to core services, or whether the process is key to the operation or supports it. If the processes are to be used as the basis for an ISO certification, then the process-oriented revision of the standards chapter should be used as the basis for the grouping. If that path is selected, there are five process groups: (1) leadership; (2) process management; (3) resource management; (4) measurement, analysis, and improvement; and (5) customer processes. For reasons of uniformity, such a structure also can be used for quality standards related to automobiles, such as QS 9000 or VDA 6.1.

The actual analysis and detailing of the processes should then be done in five steps (Fig. 4). Here, one proceeds from the general to the specific because, otherwise, the processes and links can no longer be understood due to the complexity and thus the mapping of the process fails. This is a barrier that is difficult to overcome in companies because employees generally enjoy going into detail in the process depiction and then easily become lost in these details later.

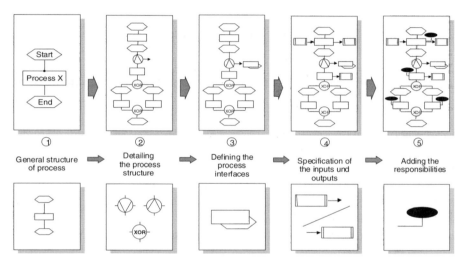

Figure 4   Flow chart for detailing the processes.

Optimizing the Processes

When the processes have been recorded, the foundation has been laid for optimization of the processes. However, during the process optimization, other initiatives that are occurring within the company at the same time—such as the introduction of self-controlling semi-autonomous groups for employee empowerment or structural changes as a consequence of reduction in the number of management levels—must also be considered. Equally, plans for the introduction of integrated enterprise systems, such as SAP or Baan, also must flow into the process view.

The goals of the process optimization generally are (1) to save resources, (2) to improve the quality of service, and/or (3) to reduce the amount of time necessary for it. Generally, the process problem areas that must be addressed are:

- *Bottlenecks*—Areas in which the work piles up because the critical path is overloaded

- *Redundancies*—Activities that are carried out several times or are performed by several different units

- *Lack of Added Value*—Unnecessary activities from the viewpoint of customer demands

- *Iterations*—Activities that are not carried out properly and therefore must be repeated

Often the process problem areas are already known, but their causes are not clear. Analyses of causes (e.g., using fishbone diagrams, spatial process analyses, or process time division) can be helpful in the diagnosis and analysis of the weak points (Fig. 5). Fishbone diagrams, for example, are suitable for analyzing causes by splitting the problem into its parts. In turn, subsections then can be formed from these parts which then systematically separate the causes of the problems. Typically, four areas are examined:

1. Methods and procedures
2. People, company culture, and unwritten laws in companies
3. Materials, information, suppliers, and other inputs
4. Machines and technical systems

Thus, for example, the problem of "long development times due to frequent changes" can originate from a lack of coordination among different organizational units (i.e., people, management) or the lack of recording of technical information from change states (i.e., machines and technical systems).

Spatial process analyses can give information on whether redundancies and iterations are present in the handling of the processes, whether long information paths are a hindrance, or whether organizational units are involved although they add no value.

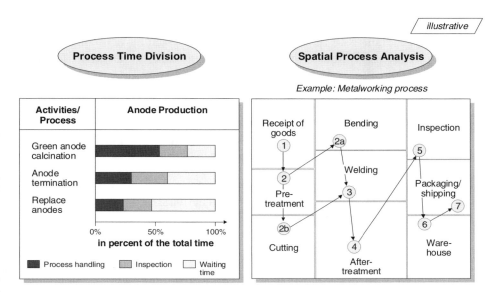

Figure 5   Process time division and spatial process analysis.

The division of the process times as another method of analysis can provide information on the time expenditure for the actual process, including any time needed for preparation, inspections, or transfer and waiting times.

Because process problem areas often have diverse causes, relationship diagrams can be used to display the cause/effect relationships. Inadequate support in a process, for example, leads to long waiting times and losses of efficiency in other processes. For example, if kanban cards from the production process do not immediately trigger withdrawal from stock or an order in Purchasing, they can be the cause of a bottleneck in production.

When the processes have been recorded and the cause/effect relationships for important weaknesses have been identified, generic methods can be used to exploit the potential for optimization:

- Processes that do not increase value or provide support to other processes should be eliminated.

- The number of interfaces among organizational units involved in a process should be reduced. This saves resources and considerably reduces the process throughput times because, for example, far less handling is necessary, wait times are eliminated, or fewer approvals are necessary.

- Drastic time advantages also can be achieved by allowing activities to run in parallel. The simultaneous engineering performed in the automobile industry is a good example of this.

- The synchronization of processes or activities can avoid the performance of redundant work. If control activities also are reduced to an acceptable level at the same time, then efficiency advantages are created.

- Processes are simplified if competencies and accountability are moved to a lower level in the hierarchy—for example, through individual empowerment or the introduction of self-controlling work groups.

- Processes run with less friction and iteration loops are avoided when intensive communication takes place on the horizontal level.

- A higher degree of standardization (e.g., through preset data templates or uniform documents, and through uniformity in the processes to be followed) leads to greater process robustness overall and thus improved quality. However, too high a degree of standardization can lead to suffocation of the spirit of innovation.

Implementing Processes

Processes can be implemented in companies when the optimized procedures are transparent for the users, and the organizational responsibilities are well defined.

The most significant factor for achieving the transparency is the availability of information regarding processes. Although the process documentation can be distributed on paper to the employees, a high degree of administrative expense is associated with controlling the processes, especially when changes are made frequently. Information management solutions—such as central server concepts or an intranet—represent relatively efficient alternatives for distributing information because they have low overall costs (Fig. 6).

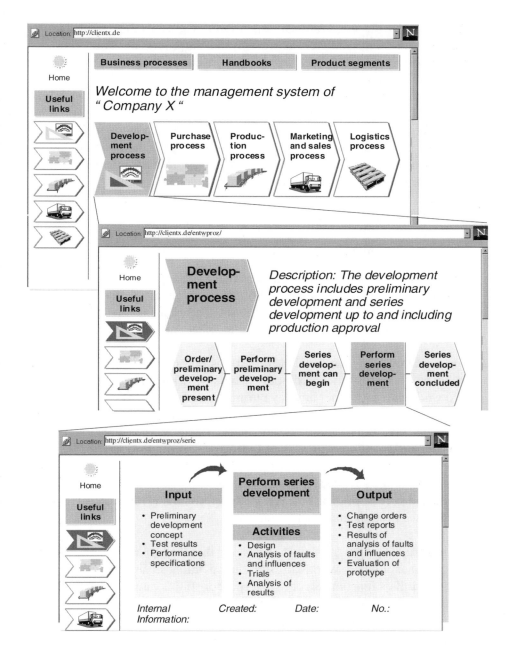

Figure 6   Intranet solution for process documentation.

With respect to the organizational responsibilities, not only the responsibility of the individuals for the different activities within the process must be defined, but also for activities in performing information functions, supporting functions, or approval functions. These are specified in responsibility profiles. These profiles define activities not for individual persons, but for roles included in the new organizational structure. If the names of persons are used, then the responsibility profiles would have to be adjusted every time a change in the staff structure takes place, which would involve increased expense. If the information from the responsibility profiles is recorded in a database, then the roles easily can be used in task descriptions as part of employee leadership. If the activity-related tasks are linked with time expenditures, then the workload can be determined to further reduce costs as a part of the task structure analysis.

Process-Change Management

An important element in the implementation of new process structures is the definition of a migration plan. This describes in detail the performance parameters, tasks, and completion milestones. This planning should include both short-term opportunities as well as long-term, often visionary, company goals.

The migration plan should include three transition steps: (1) a flexible project organization loosely anchored in the company, (2) forming teams of people who work with each other anyway during the daily business, and, finally, (3) the modification of the company structure organization (Fig. 7). The number of persons involved increases steadily in each step. At the beginning, a small team of employees, who are assigned to the project full time, takes care of the change process. During the course of change management, more and more agents of change are added—people who maintain their line functions. Only a specified portion of their time (typically approximately 20 percent) is dedicated to the process implementation.

During project planning, it must be ensured that the line management, which typically has a heavy workload from the operating businesses, has enough time to fulfill its function as coach and sponsor. If this cannot be assured, then the change process can easily be held up.

To check progress, a detailed milestone plan has proven to be absolutely necessary because such a plan establishes the individual steps that are needed in the process implementation. However, care must be taken not to go

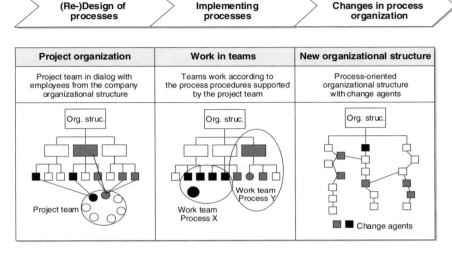

Figure 7   Successive transition of organizational forms.

overboard in getting people to fulfill the technical requirements or produce documents. The factors in the change process which are sometimes described as "soft" also should be considered. This includes factors such as desired changes in attitudes, increasing identification with the project goal, or the formation of learning effects. If these aspects are ignored, then the process optimization may become merely another academic exercise.

A complex change process is required in many areas and at different levels if a holistic change in the company thinking from a functional to a process orientation is to be successful in the long run. It is difficult to find the right approach to successfully start the change process using only a variety of adjustment levers in an unplanned way. Therefore, one of the key questions that frequently is asked is: In what section of the company should the change process start?

Organizational Aspects of the Process-Change Concept

If the change process is initiated with people responsible for a core performance process, who are used to process thinking in any case, then rapid results follow. In the background is the existence of product or service which will be achieved at the end of the process. This represents an easy orientation point in the examination of the process flow and serves as the criteria for determining the success of the business. In this situation, the necessary measurement criteria and control instruments for checking and maintaining the efficiency of the processes are relatively easy to identify. Data such as waiting time, throughput time, or error rates also are often standard data recorded for controlling, which can be applied to the core performance process with slight modifications. Complex software for process modeling also can aid in the evaluation of the data.

The danger of the introduction of process orientation that is limited merely to people involved in the core performance processes is obvious: the accompanying support processes, which are equally important for overall success, then are not attended to nearly as much as necessary. This is true because the people responsible for these support processes usually are in administrative departments and have a more difficult time seeing the overall effects of their activities, especially their connection to the core performance processes, because of their minimal involvement in the product. An adaptation of process thinking on their part is much more difficult to achieve. When the change process is not handled simultaneously, the interfaces between supporting and core performance processes are not attended to sufficiently. A company will achieve process orientation only when the interface problems are overcome.

Capacity problems and the complexity of the change make a simultaneous rollout of the change process in all parts of the company very difficult. Old departmental structures with their fixed sets of tasks are broken up and partially replaced by new organizational units. Individual units should pave the way as leaders with their relevant processes so that the initial difficulties involved in the change do not end in tangled confusion, with plenty of irritated employees. They must be quickly followed by the others so that the rollout does not suffer from any longer breaks or, worst of all, come to a stop.

Often the only possible way is a compromise between sequential and simultaneous progress. This has proven to be the most sensible method of proceeding in the beginning of the change process needed to instill a process-oriented company philosophy.

The change process then continues to proceed to cover the entire company in a process comparable to cell division. A one-way, top-down approach alone does not seem promising because it would appear to be a program task forced upon the employees by the management. Also, the departmental egotism previously mentioned cannot be completely eliminated with this form of transition. Another requirement for success is an accompanying introduction of a communication program which at first generates initial interest and attention at the lower levels of an organization and later the will to change by demonstrating the advantages of the change.

The integration of this accompanying communications program in an improvement program that has already been successfully established in the company has proven to be very helpful and leads to saving of resources. These programs are usually quite broad and present a good forum to present the process concept to the employees. The connection of the process optimization with, for example, the total quality initiative in the company shows employees what advantages they and the company obtain from optimally structured and executed processes—for example, the time savings in process handling. Other examples of good compatibility of process orientation with other projects are preparation for certification for ISO or VDA standards, continual improvement programs, and also newly introduced leadership approaches such as empowerment principles or the learning organization.

Process Performance Measurement as an Introductory and Later as a Control Instrument

It can be seen again and again that incentive and control systems related to the processes often are the most effective way to get employees to pursue the change process and to turn it into a process philosophy that they embody. For example, as soon as Purchasing is no longer primarily concerned only with filling all of the spaces and carefully administering the orders but also with reducing throughput time and errors in the core performance process of the product manufacture and delivery, the attitudes toward its activities and interfaces change. The product program planner, previously viewed as an "enemy" from the other side because he needs everything very quickly and in variable quantities, now becomes a helpful coordination partner who helps contribute to keeping the entire process friction-free and optimized. Successes of one functional department then positively affect other departments in the company because they are linked to each other in the process chain.

Process performance measurements are helpful in three dimensions, depending on the degree of maturity of the process:

- To check the efficiency of original tasks and processes (e.g., with regard to cost and throughput or reaction times)

- To check the general efficiency of the redesigned processes

- To check the robustness of the new processes

The processes recorded in their original forms—that is, the way in which they existed in the company before any attempts were made to improve them— are improved by the methods described under "optimization of the processes." The results usually can be measured by concrete savings figures, for example, related to process time or process cost.

To check the general efficiency of a process that has already been redesigned or optimized, one should use elements of cost and performance analysis, supplemented by indicators related to time and quality factors. So-called "balanced scorecards" can supply the methodological basis for performance measure-based controlling. They deliver the link between the vision and the strategy of a company on the one hand, and the process-oriented performance measures on the other hand. Balanced scorecards help formulate variables for measurement and control on the basis of strategy and process.

This form of process performance measurement is repetitive, in contrast to one previously mentioned, and the target figures for the next evaluation period are based in part on knowledge of historical data. Depending on the process documentation program selected, the average costs, throughput times, or error rates for individual processes can be determined using simulations. If there are alternative procedures within the process, they can be optimized using the analysis of the performance measurement. In contrast to the classic activity-based costing, the activities and process steps can be analyzed in their overall context on a transparent basis.

The third dimension of performance measurement checks how closely the real operations in the company follow the documented processes.

If the process shows many variations or if it deviates from its documented version, then a couple of actions must be taken. First, the deviations must be examined for interpretation with respect to the optimal process flow. In some cases, this will lead to changes in the process map. Second, the employees must be shown and trained to ensure that the entire process is deployed in the best possible way.

Typical Barriers on the Path to Change

Implementing change is not a continuous process, but an up-and-down roller-coaster ride with some successes and many obstacles and setbacks. The skeptics in the company are always quick to react. They quickly get the conservative majority of the employees on their side with arguments that point out dangers to the individual and their carefully worked-out positions and privileges. Any holes in the implementation concept, which can occur even in the best plan, are described as weaknesses in the system and are taken as proof that the new system does not lead to a better way for conducting business. They argue that the good old process should be maintained because "it has always worked."

Problems arise when employees who are completely ignorant about the change receive this news. This is true because not every employee will be included in the concept and the initial implementation phase. Many—usually most of the employees—are introduced to the change process when their actual duties change, either because of the process orientation or changes in their own processes. If the change agents have not laid the groundwork and have not generated interest and understanding for the situation and the task, then a barrier may easily be created. The conversion of the processes is then seen as something that is forced on them, a senseless exercise by management.

If the process optimization occurs in combination with the introduction of a new IT system (e.g., the introduction of enterprise systems such as SAP or Baan), then adjustments should be made regularly. Because no process is geared toward 100-percent adaptation throughout the firm, such adjustments are necessary to ensure that the programs will actually be used. If such adjustments are not made, then it is easy to voice criticism that is usually difficult to dismiss. In fact, there are cases in which one has to ask: Is the company optimizing its processes, or is it adapting to suit the new IT system? Here, those responsible for the processes must ensure that they are truly set up for efficiency rather than ease of handling with the IT system. This is also the reason why the customizing of enterprise systems and the introduction of process orientation should not be done at the same time by the same person; otherwise, the advantages of process optimization and orientation will not really pay off.

How to display a process and to what degree of detail should it be described are examples of problems in the change process. The acceptance of the processes, meaning thereby the readiness to perform them according to the guidelines and "to live them," depends greatly on whether they are useful for everyday business and are understandable for everyone concerned. Here, however, one often runs into conflicts of interest, and thus compromises are necessary in the selection of the documentation software. For example, the criteria for clarity, understandability, and transparency can come into conflict with criteria such as "suitability for a relational database" or "ability to run a flow simulation."

If one permits limitations on the criteria of clarity and understandability, then difficulties in process depictions or descriptions of activities arise. The activities may become described in language that is different from that used in practice. This quickly leads to non-acceptance of the documents: "Too theoretical" is the reason often heard. Typically, such problems arise when one depends too much on the IT-oriented reference models of the enterprise systems. The actual business procedures in the company then are relegated to the background. Supposedly nit-picky issues such as these lead to major obstacles and loss of time when pursuing the change process.

How can obstacles be quickly and permanently cleared away?

The plan for handling obstacles should ideally be laid out in the implementation phase. However, this is not enough. After all, presence of relevant documentation and clear definition of the organizational responsibilities are nothing more than a framework.

Within the transformation process, the time expenditure for change agents becomes discontinuous. In the "normal" situation in companies today, all key figures in the company are overworked; therefore, typically the tasks that require strategic or change duties are relegated to "when time is available."

This behavior, which results in many of the problems previously described here, can be countered when the operative requirements are defined in preparing the project schedule, and a certain percentage of the individual and team work time is reserved for transformation tasks from the start. The necessity for delegation resulting from this has a side effect in that it breaks up functional hierarchies and promotes self-determination. If the transition is successful, then a portion of the overwork disappears because the causes of overwork, such as waiting time and redundant work, disappear.

Another source of problems is the technical support for implementation of the processes. Because only a few will remain with the process optimization throughout its course, technical knowledge to carry out the changes often is lacking. The building of a task force whose members see themselves as technically specialized process experts can help the change agents in the various departments as needed. This will take care of a common problem that although the change agent is willing and would be in the position to implement the change, he lacks the necessary technical (process-relevant) competence to do so, in spite of introduction to the topic and becoming trained as a change agent. This is where the task force experts are needed. They can provide support for contents and methodical development, especially because they usually are released from much of their normal work responsibilities to serve for such special duties.

The approaches to process optimization used to be described as mechanistic. The modern approach recognizes the human element in the process of change. Individuals have a decisive effect on all four adjustment levers in the optimization cycle—from the task of process mapping, to the often long and difficult change process. Among all of the technical difficulties and disputes over contents, one should not forget the human aspects of those affected by the change.

On What Does Success Depend?

Process re-engineering consistently carried out has many significant consequences. It leads to altered processes, different organizational structures, new information technology systems, and a changed company culture. Experience has shown that the success of such a plan often depends on a few important factors. These are:

1. Top-down leadership

2. Intensive and broadly based communication to ensure that no mistrust arises among employees

3. Early focus on concrete processes and subprocesses

4. Determining clear, aggressive goals for reorganization with reference to customer benefits

5. Use of clear implementation organization with "hard" milestones in the migration planning

6. Open learning from other organizations (e.g., through benchmarking)

7. Making allowances for the company culture

8. Making competency and capacity available to change a large number of people

9. Use of modern information and communications technology

10. Initiating implementation early and in clearly visible pieces

Finally, successful process-orientation can be created only when the entire staff is behind it and lives by processes as a matter of common company practice. The change must be based on convictions.

Literature

Feige, A., and Wolters, H., "Entwicklung: Der Schlüssel zum Überleben," in *Automobil Entwicklung–Design–Technologie*, September 1997, pp. 132–134.
Garvin, D., "Leveraging Processes for Strategic Advantage: A Roundtable with Xerox's Allaire, USAA's Herres, SmithKline Beecham's Leschly, and Pepsi's Weatherup," in *Harvard Business Review*, September/October 1995.
Hoyle, D., *QS-9000 Quality Systems Handbook*, Newton, MA, 1997.

Kaplan, R., and Norton, D., "Using the Balanced Scorecard as a Strategic Management System," in *Harvard Business Review*, January/February 1996, pp. 75–85.

Majchrzak, A., and Wang, Q., "Breaking Functional Mindset in Process Organizations," in *Harvard Business Review*, September/October 1996, pp. 93–99.

Scott-Morgan, P., *The Unwritten Rules of the Game: Master Them, Shatter Them, and Break Through the Barriers to Organizational Change*, New York, 1994.

"Best Practice" Through Empowerment and Process-Oriented Management

Jean-Christophe Deslarzes, Laurent Forestier

> *To change an organization, the more people you can involve*
> *and the faster you can help them understand how the system works*
> *and how to take responsibility for making it work better,*
> *the faster will be the change.*
> —Marvin Weisbord

Rapid change has become an ever-present challenge in business. New trends must be monitored constantly so that the threat of competition can be met. No company can escape this essential process of change. To master the ability to change, all of the company resources must be mobilized, especially the human resources. Only those companies that promote all of the skills and initiative their staff has to offer can succeed. After all, a company is nothing but a collection of individuals, all of whom must contribute their personal strengths and abilities.

Participation of each and every employee in implementing the company strategy and goals, improving its organization, and updating its culture is the basis of success. Greater sense of responsibility, autonomy, and willingness, coupled with clearly targeted working processes therefore are essential to respond to the growing complexity of organizations today. How to achieve the objective of having increasingly contented staff working in successful organizations is one of the greatest challenges for management. Let us examine how our firm, Alusuisse, has coped with this challenge.

Alusuisse in Times of Change

Alusuisse Schweizerische Aluminium AG, Sierre is a subsidiary of the globally active Lonza Group (algroup). The company headquarters are in Wallis, Switzerland. Approximately 1,600 staff are employed at three plants in Sierre, Chippis, and Steg. The company's activities include all stages of aluminum production— from electrolysis to the manufacture of semi-finished products. With its almost 100 years of experience, Alusuisse is one of the major European suppliers in the pressing and rolling field. Our company has earned an international reputation in such diverse areas as railway wagon production, shipbuilding, and mechanical and electrical engineering. In the automotive industry field, we supply bodywork pressings for Audi and Rover, among others.

We experienced a financial crisis in the early 1990s. Major losses were incurred, mainly due to spectacular price declines for raw metals. As a result, the company was restructured, which unfortunately also involved reducing staff by approximately 25 percent. In 1995, the company showed a profit for the first time after five years of losses. In the years that followed, our profitability further increased. Improvement in the general market situation and a relatively stable metal price undoubtedly played an important role in our success. However, the main cause is to be found in our customer orientation, constant willingness to innovate, reduction of internal costs, and introduction of novel working procedures such as empowerment, as well as a process-oriented management system.

An empowerment program was introduced worldwide by algroup in 1995, with the aim of making our working organization more flexible, cutting hierarchies, and enforcing process orientation. Empowerment is meant to motivate our staff to greater performance by delegating greater responsibility for decisions downward. Alusuisse began using self-managing working teams (SATs) as part of this program.

In 1996, the company decided to change its information technology by introducing SAP R/3. This system was planned for all departments and was required to be up and running within only two years of the project being started. We hoped for process-oriented integration of all departments using the SAP modules and, above all, for cost reductions in the medium term. This timetable was met, and our company now operates with SAP R/3, although many improvements are still needed.

In February 1997, we had to renew our ISO 9001 certification. Certification testing success indicated that we needed a process-oriented management system. We had introduced our SATs as part of the empowerment program, designed them around defined working processes, and adapted the SAP modules to our company culture in a process-oriented manner. It was now of the utmost importance that we achieved coherence among all of these processes and methods. These projects, although focused on specific sequences, functioned on the basis of differing premises when dealing with processes. We therefore decided to coalesce all of our working sequences under a single process-oriented management system and strive for the appropriate process-oriented ISO 9001 and 14001 certification in March 1999.

How our empowerment project was designed and set up is detailed here next, followed by information on the process-oriented management system. This chapter ends with some remarks on current results and some conclusions.

The Way to Empowerment

In the early 1980s, European industry concentrated primarily on the sequences and productivity of machinery. Later, it was recognized that the staff attending plant can increase productivity as part of quality circles if the group provides important solutions. Since the end of the 1980s, companies increasingly are giving staff more responsibility and training them in preventive and autonomous management techniques. Total Quality Management (TQM) was then complemented step-by-step by other management techniques such as *Kaizen* and Total Productive Maintenance. Today, industry does not concentrate solely on the quality of its goods and services but on maximizing overall company performance using Economical Value Added (EVA) techniques.

Alusuisse began to use SATs in 1995 as a part of its empowerment program. These are made up of staff who assume responsibilities and require minimal managerial control on a daily basis in the workplace. Using SATs wherever justifiable means that we have the best possible method in our hands for passing on to our staff responsibility for decisions, media, information, and authority, thus creating for them more influence on their own work.

SAT members are responsible for their own work, decide their own timetables and working plans, make decisions concerning production and/or service, set their own personal goals, and autonomously solve their problems. They also organize team meetings, analyze and improve working procedures, and coordinate work with other teams, suppliers, and clients. Until recently, working groups took responsibility only for their directly delegated tasks. Now, since the introduction of empowerment, the team members are responsible for the entire departmental process. The individual employee does not perform only his or her own core duties. Each person also deals with a comprehensive field of responsibility together with the other team members.

In contrast with traditional linear organization, the SATs work on a client-orientated basis and less on a basis of orientation to the next higher level in the hierarchy. SAT membership generally is interdisciplinary in composition and manages itself. The teams also participate in intensive communication activity.

The hindrances to success in company change, especially a change of the working method in SATs, are numerous. Approximately 70 percent of companies contemplating such change fail to achieve it. This is mainly due to three reasons:

- First, planning often is carried out on the basis of handbooks or manuals and remains purely theoretical, without taking adequate account of specific company circumstances.

- Second, lack of courage in making change leads to retention of the old procedures and methods.

- Third, managers often put their faith in traditional solutions, even if new situations demand innovative answers.

When introducing SAT, work within the organization may initially seem chaotic compared to the old situation. Dismantling rigid structures is actually conducive to staff creativity and flexibility. Transition from a traditional to an SAT organization may result in disorder if the change is pushed too hard and important implementation phases are neglected. It is a fantasy to believe that a company can be restructured in SATs from one day to the next. Alusuisse therefore applied empowerment within the company in five phases. Three years after starting the project, we currently plan on at least another three years being needed to complete the change in company culture.

Clear Targets

To formulate clear goals and tasks for the empowerment project, it was necessary to learn from other companies. We set up six teams, defined by operating departments, to visit innovative companies. We then more precisely defined the tasks to be completed and developed a five-phase schedule with clearly defined milestones.

In the first phase, goals and scope of the new working method and the costs to be expected were laid down precisely. This is important, because it is essential to have a clear idea of the goals and the effects of empowerment before beginning the project. In the course of brainstorming sessions, the Alusuisse managerial team came to comprehend the current situation in the company in all respects and had to reach to a consensus on its vision of the company's future. We had to consider the advantages as well as the costs and risks that are associated with a change in organization and mentality. We reached the conclusion that we would be more innovative as a result of empowerment, might save costs, could supply our clients more quickly with the goods and services ordered, and could offer them the desired high-quality products at the desired time. Our staff should not view these goals as a fad but as strategic company direction. However, it was difficult initially to make it clear to them how and why empowerment would improve our competitive position on the market.

Mobilization of Management and Supervisors

We view the change in state of mind and behavior on the part of our management staff and supervisors as one of the prime factors in the success of our change to SAT organization. Team-oriented behavior cannot be expected of any employee unless his or her superiors demonstrate this philosophy, too.

In general, middle management and supervisors feel frustrated at losing sole control of their work processes. Management often sees itself as expert in its own specialized field and fears losing this status if the responsibilities of subordinates increase.

Thus, it was not surprising that individual managers and supervisors in our company feared they would lose the rights they had well earned over the years. Others thought that empowerment would plunge our company into chaos. We identified four potential major barriers to successful change:

1. Poor definition of the new role of management and/or supervisors

2. The feeling of those affected that they will lose status and/or authority

3. Fear that the new organization might result in unemployment

4. Immediate superiors not being able to provide support or be role models

We sensed that our management and supervisors would be most resistant to the change to empowerment. Therefore, it was important for us to make those responsible for the teams in the past and future become aware of the subject and be sensitive to it. We wanted them to understand the project, accept it, and back it without hesitation. This was achieved in two stages. First, the management in every plant was informed of the project and its goals. The information meetings held for that purpose were run by the project manager and the appropriate departmental manager. In the second stage, external consultants and experts in motivation training were used to train the supervisors. A year later, team formation training was conducted. This matter will be further discussed in the section on "Success Factors and Lessons." Personality tests revealed to us the strengths and weaknesses of each supervisor needing to be considered in setting up the content of this training.

The goal in this stage was to convince those particularly critical of the project (both management and supervisors) of the importance of the success of the project. In the case of some managerial staff—fortunately, a minority—this was a long process because they were fundamentally opposed to change within the company as a matter of principle.

Mobilization of the Entire Staff

In this third stage, we comprehensively informed all staff of the goals and content of empowerment. Various techniques were used to do so, including information meetings in departments with approximately 500 staff each, discussions in smaller groups, articles in the company newspaper and local press, and use of humorous posters in the workplace.

A staff contentment analysis confirmed that our staff in some departments looked forward to the new philosophy with confidence. The first SATs therefore were set up very quickly to ensure that we could refer to positive results garnered by the new working methods and thus motivate the remaining staff. We also organized training after setting up the first SATs with the special theme of teamwork, which was followed by regular coaching for the teams and "animators" (the term we selected for the team leaders). (Please refer to the section on "Success Factors and Lessons.") A lot of energy had to be invested in realizing these first SATs because their success as role models was of paramount importance. Subsequently, the numerous SATs were set up and the performance of each was regularly communicated to the staff in the company newspaper. These examples of success helped reduce the resistance of the remaining staff, and they were successfully mobilized toward empowerment.

Reconsideration of the Company Structures and Working Procedures

In the next step, working procedures and organization were analyzed, and some changes were made. This was effectively the transition phase in which new SATs were constantly being formed. On the surface, this was merely a quick process analysis involving staff participation. However, the decisive question of upon which working procedure the SATs should individually be based also was included in this analysis. It became clear that in some departments, processes and spheres of responsibility would have to be redefined so that a basis for empowerment could be found. Process documentation as part of a process-oriented management system was drafted against this background. (Please refer to the section on the "Process-Oriented Management System.") This empowerment transition from a functional to a market- and process-oriented philosophy also allowed us to flatten the hierarchical structure.

Continuous Improvement

After the teams had been composed and trained, they were constantly supported. In this phase, the personnel strategy was reconsidered, and methods that were slowing the project were adapted to the philosophy.

Even today, we continue to simplify procedures and rules as part of an ongoing process. In our company culture, which is based on mutual trust, not every activity can be constrained by rigid rules and regulations. Regular training talks also must be held, although some supervisors have not begun doing so on more than an irregular basis.

Our company pay policy also has been brought into line with empowerment. Since 1997, a team bonus system has replaced the old individual bonus system. One cannot make team performance the prime consideration and, at the same time, reward staff achievements individually. The unwritten rules of individual achievement would then contradict the written rules based on teamwork.

The individual specifications of tasks and duties within the so-called "team responsibility profile" also must change. They must emphasize the cooperation of team members with one another and reflect the relationships with suppliers as well as both internal and external clients. The responsibility profiles are in alignment with process documentation. (Please refer to the section on the "Process-Oriented Management System.") Thus, adhering to responsibility profiles ensures process-oriented working methods. The SATs must have adequate performance measures to ensure that they constantly improve themselves. Our new team bonus system may be the best way of checking the development of the SATs because it is based on a maximum of four appropriate components. These are produced quantity, quality, logistics, and safety/orderliness/cleanliness. A higher bonus is given if the performance measures exceed the plan.

The development of an SAT is charted using the so-called "team development table" (Fig. 1). The horizontal axis of the table shows the names of the team working within a particular production facility or department. The vertical axis shows the four development phases of SATs with their related activities. The team members are to master the activities within the phase in which they are working. The team receives a black dot for every activity it masters, a green dot for each activity that is partially mastered, and a blank if the activity is not expected to be a part of the team's skill set. These team development tables are drafted and maintained by each team's internal coach working with the team members. Because the coaches usually are members of the empowerment project team, the objectivity of the tables becomes the responsibility of the team. This measurement chart is posted at the entrance of

	Start	Team								

Phase I: Introduction

Definition of 1 or 2 own goals per team with the support of the cadre
Organization of the infrastructure (place of meeting bulletin board)
Understanding/knowledge of the empowerment philosophy
Hold team meetings
Solve conflicts between team members (with support)
Etc.

Phase II: Transition to new way of working

Original, independent definition of 1 or 2 goals per team
Original use of methods to solve problems and conflicts
Knowledge and understanding of performance indicators
Decisions are made in the team
Active cooperation with the support services (development, quality)
Etc.

Phase III: Experiences

Determination of goals of the team based on the goals of the company with support
Following the performance indicators and the goals
Planning and coordination with other teams (deadlines, projects, personnel)
Participation of the team in the training of new team members
Organization and planning of the current support of the machines
Etc.

Phase IV: Progress

Original determination of goals for the team based on the goals of the company
Annual feedback to every member of the entire team
Selection of new team members (total work contract)
Increase in versatility within the team
Definition of criteria for continual improvement
Etc.

☐ Not begun   ▨ Partially mastered   ■ Mastered

Figure 1   Team development table.

183

every facility and is intended to help an SAT self-evaluate its progress. The chart also is a valuable tool for the empowerment project management and team, as well as for managerial staff supporting the SATs.

Success Factors and Lessons

Successful change to SATs, with accompanying cultural change, depends (in our experience) on a number of factors:

- Staff must trust managers and supervisors.

- Team members, managers, and supervisors must be well aware of what is expected of them in future.

- Staff must be open to change.

- Management and staff must have no fear of loss of status.

- Management must actively develop a strongly participatory managerial culture and integrate staff in major decision making.

- Management must support change and assume a role model function.

The following three activities were of major importance to the success of our project.

1. *Decentralized project teams*—The conditions at each specific location were reflected in team composition in terms of participation of different disciplines of engineering, language, and culture. We also installed as many change agents (approximately 60) as possible, as quickly as possible.

   First, we ensured that management and supervisory staff were represented in these teams. It was important that they have a clearer understanding of the performance goal and the way to achieve it than that expected from other staff. The next step immediately thereafter was integrating workers in the project teams to create multifunctional and hierarchically autonomous team structures representing all staff during the project.

We considered the formation of teams as a critical part of the project. A centralized group would not have complied with the SAT philosophy or led to the rapid successes that the project committee could show. However, we now find that approximately half of the project teams have become dormant. For several months, they have not managed to take any concrete action such as supporting the newly introduced SATs, improving communications and cooperation among SATs, or generally promoting a harmonious atmosphere. This is the result of additional cost due to our SAP project and very positive increases in orders. In addition, and this may be the main reason, the initial enthusiasm and energy associated with it has slackened somewhat. We currently are applying appropriate corrective measures such as improved support from project management and restaffing of some project teams to ensure that they have renewed creativity, motivation, and enthusiasm.

2. *Training and coaching*—Training gives our management and team animators the necessary means to master the switch from a culture based on command structure to one based on cooperation. Each animator must learn to become a coach. This means that they must be able to, for example, eradicate barriers, find properly thought-out answers, act as clients' friends, and be role models for empowerment. The basis of all team animator training is a set of questionnaires, completed anonymously by colleagues and subordinates, that comprehensively covers animators' social skills. These give animators an exact picture of how they are evaluated by those around them. Participants complete their training with a clear definition of their personal goals and how to achieve them.

A similar method is used to prepare the team members to fulfill their new role within the team. They become capable of independently running team meetings efficiently, receiving and transmitting feedback, solving problems in the team, making decisions by teamwork, agreeing on goals, measuring results, planning activities, and settling conflicts within the team. Again, the training is based on questionnaires anonymously completed by the team. Team members individually submit their personal opinions on the efficiency and harmony of a team, and the coach bases training specifically on these opinions. Various exercises to simulate teamwork are undertaken with the aim of making participants aware of the advantages of using the tools in their daily work. For this purpose, our teams spend two days together in a mountain chalet. The team members plan the journey together, organize the catering, receive training on teamwork on the first day, and then put that knowledge to practice during an outdoor exercise on the second day. The teams are coached every two to six months by the consultant(s) who initially trained them. Furthermore, every SAT has a member of the project team available as an internal consultant. The teams are supported in this way to ensure that the list of problems they identified can be coupled with a plan of action and their performance continuously improved.

3. *Process transparency*—We are convinced that empowerment can achieve its goals only if processes within the company are aligned and a clear organizational structure is created. This is why our organizational structure is based on function (e.g., marketing, production) and in alignment with market and processes.

How this process-oriented management system was introduced is detailed next.

Process-Oriented Management System

Two years after introducing empowerment—one year after the introduction of SAP, one year before the renewal of ISO 9001 certification and together with the new ISO 14001 certification—it became apparent that the current projects would need to be dealt with using process orientation. This is because the two main projects in our company—empowerment and SAP—on the surface represent two fundamentally different philosophies. While empowerment mainly emphasizes work organization, SAP focuses on information technology sequences to which humans must adapt. Some staff members had difficulty in recognizing the association between the two, in view of these differences. To coalesce the two projects and coordinate the processes involved, our company decided to implement a process-oriented management system. This was applied in six stages, as shown in Fig. 2.

As Alusuisse understands it, a process means key company activities that are organized according to a set sequence. This always formally includes an initial activity setting the process in motion and a final activity to reach an end condition. The interim activities are linked in a logical sequence.

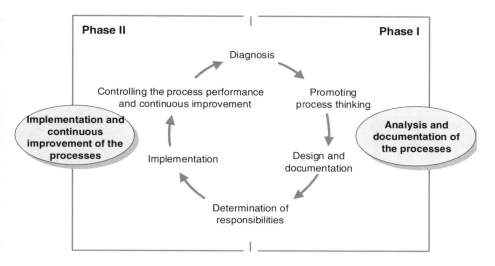

Figure 2   The circulatory process sequence.

When a process project is mentioned, one thinks initially of re-engineering (i.e., radical change to processes). The frequently unstated goal of this type of project is to cut costs, mainly by reducing staff. In Alusuisse, however, a process-based project involves first identifying the key processes used by staff and then structuring them in a standardized form. Staff are then responsible for managing their own processes and optimizing them to ensure continuous improvement.

Keeping that in mind, the project group entrusted with applying the process philosophy as discussed here was composed of staff from Quality Control, Personnel, Environmental Protection, Accounting, and Logistics. It also seemed essential to have the entire top management participate to ensure that the project had the necessary backing in implementation and management. Also, doing so made it possible to make the necessary decisions quickly. Including top management is a step that cannot be omitted because it directly affects acceptance of the project by staff and the speed at which the project can be introduced. Furthermore, process owners were nominated and assigned the task of structuring current processes and refining them, as well as defining the spheres of responsibility within each process. More than 50 people responsible for projects were integrated in the project group. Thanks to their expertise and experience, the project was concluded successfully.

Record of the Status Quo

We decided to establish three process-structuring groups responsible for strategic processes, operational processes, and supportive processes. The strategic processes cover all activities associated with medium- and long-term strategic decisions, such as drafting a business plan for five years, setting up various budgets and conducting external communication, providing administration of major projects, and performing analysis of customer satisfaction. Operational processes include all activities directly associated with the operational value chain of our products. Such processes mesh into one another and thus form an integrated production process. In the case of client-to-client processes, this begins with product and procedure development and continues through tender drafting, order processing, production planning, production, packaging, and shipment to invoicing and processing complaints. This list mentions only the most important activities. In addition, support processes exist which cover all activities associated with adding value to our products, such as maintenance, accounting, information technology, quality assurance, logistics, purchasing, personnel, and SGU (safety, health, and the environment).

Alusuisse had some documented processes before the project began, as a direct consequence of ISO 9001 certification in 1991. This documentation, however, was too detailed in part because it was primarily concerned with production processes and, within those, almost exclusively with engineering matters. The activity sequences also were difficult to understand, and different presentation methods often were used. In the strategic and support areas, in particular, the existing procedures were rarely shown in the form of processes.

Promoting Process Thinking

The process documentation was drafted with the aid of numerous conferences, meetings, and workshops with the process owners. The main challenges were related to the existence, justification, and form of future processes. Many staff initially questioned the need for, and the purpose of, such a process philosophy and the approach associated with it. This was, after all, the third major project in only three years. Others needed time to adapt before becoming acquainted with the layout of the logical process sequences. Whether the process philosophy would permit alignment of the different existing projects also was doubted.

The term "philosophy" is of critical importance because in both process orientation and empowerment, what is involved is, above all, a change in behavior in daily work and hence a change in company culture. Although the enthusiasm of our staff was not great when the project began, the first examples of success due to process orientation had a positive influence on everyone involved in the work process.

Design and Documentation

Design and documentation of the process was conducted in several stages, the first of which consisted of drafting a simple list of activities with the aid of process owners. These activities were then structured logically in the form of a sequence. The final stage was drafting the process with clearly identified inputs and outputs, as well as relationships to other processes in the company. These inputs and outputs of a process represent the information received from other processes (input) and that sent to other processes (output). The inputs and outputs were the most difficult to draft because several divisions were affected. (This is exactly why successfully linking the appropriate interfaces with one another is so important.)

A large-scale workshop was organized in which all managers affected by the project participated, all the way up to the chairman of the board. The total attendance was approximately 70 people. Each person had an opportunity during the workshop to have other participants mention the inputs they needed and the outputs they had to pass on. Numerous superfluous and useless inputs and outputs were scrapped. This workshop was a turning point in developing the project because the 100 processes displayed on the wall of the meeting room showed every participant the importance of cooperation within and among the processes. The importance of acting across divisions and in alignment with natural work processes became clear.

The required coherence between process and SAP projects became obvious to everyone involved during this phase of documentation. We documented all operational processes and, wherever possible, the support process according to SAP module implementation. This was difficult for the strategic processes, however, because they were not included in SAP and had to be developed "from scratch." We chose a uniform method for process design with the aid of

ARISToolset software. This program, specially designed for process sequences, is not user friendly but has the advantage of linking activities within a clearly structured database.

The choice of a new form of display also changed our documentation for ISO 9001. The twenty chapters prescribed in our old quality handbook were transformed into seven chapters in a management handbook, one of which covered the documented processes.

Determining Spheres of Responsibility

Defining a process is one thing. Having it brought to life by the user is at least as difficult. The first step in this direction is to determine process ownership. Someone must be accountable for each process, one who possesses the necessary expertise and ability to take responsibility for a process within the framework of our new philosophy.

The process owner's initial role was to draft the process on the basis of the activities list. As soon as this was done, the process of adding inputs and outputs was conducted. Subsequently, the role of the process owner was to keep the process updated. This, of course, remains the case. The owner also must nominate the staff responsible for the relevant activities within the process. In visualizing a process, it generally is obvious which persons need to cooperate within the framework of a process, regardless of the department or division in the company to which they belong. We included this activities list and the list of responsible persons in a table called the "Responsibility Profile" (Fig. 3).

This table links the activities of the processes with the functions responsible for performing them. Where vertical and horizontal lines meet in the table, the tasks coded RASI (Responsibility, Agreement, Support, and Information) are more closely defined. Stating the function(s) rather than the name of the person(s) responsible permits us the necessary flexibility when organizational changes occur and avoids the need to change the table every time such an event occurs. Currently defined individual specifications of duties and responsibilities are replaced by these profiles in the case of all staff involved in a key process who work within a team. They now can determine

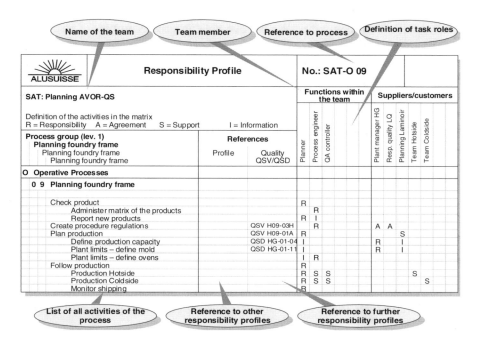

Figure 3   Matrix for defining spheres of responsibility.

relationships to working instructions. Although the role of empowerment is to give staff new responsibility within team structures, we have now aligned empowerment and processes via team responsibility profiles.

Implementation

As processes constantly develop, we are considering abandoning paper communications. Currently, an intranet solution is being designed—permitting, by a mere mouse click, an instant visualization of any process and the associated responsibility profile by any staff member at the workplace. This is absolutely essential to creating transparency. Furthermore, the version of a document that appears on the intranet is always the latest.

Another major advantage of the intranet is the option of linking documents with one another, regardless of the computer on which these documents are located within the company. We believe we can greatly improve, structure, and modernize the newly created processes using documents that were already available. Thanks to our intranet, our processes—which in paper form risked disappearing permanently in a drawer—will be changed into a living "organism" that adapts and improves automatically to reflect company changes. Finally, the fact that such vital information is only a mouse click away will popularize the great advantages of the intranet.

Monitoring Process Performance and Constant Improvement

The only means of measuring process efficiency is to define indices and compare achieved values with the target data established. Meeting targets guarantees the success of the process in the given period. The task of defining these indices must not be neglected. Poor selection of indices may give a false picture of the performance and capacity of a process. Only a limited number of such indices should be defined to avoid information over-load. The indices must be extrapolated from company goals and targets (Fig. 4).

Drafting these indices is the last joint task for process owners and the project team. Only on the basis of measured values can process owners monitor the

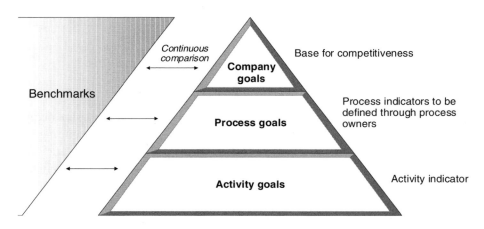

Figure 4 Determining process indices.

functionality of their process. They must then decide on the need for corrective measures as soon as they discover that performance is below target.

The circle of constant improvement is closed as the process owner takes corrective measures to fix problems, defines new goals, changes the process appropriately, redefines responsibilities, and measures process capacity and performance anew.

Success Factors and Lessons Learned

Successful implementation of our project is due primarily to three factors:

- A key success factor has been the process-oriented management system that permits major projects, empowerment, and SAP to be linked with a common philosophy. The principle of "team responsibility profiles" is extracted directly from the empowerment project and has been applied in part already. In presenting the processes, we included structure and syntax of SAP in our considerations. Thanks to process orientation, our staff are able to rely on a new language and philosophy common to all, regardless of division. Communications among divisions has improved, making greater transparency possible and increasing efficiency.

- Assumption of responsibility for drafting and updating processes and responsibility profiles by process owners certainly is another major success factor. It would have been inappropriate to subject the persons affected to processes they did not create and thus put in question their expertise on internal sequences and procedures. By giving them a major role in the process design, we ensured that the process definition will survive. Possible rejection of documented processes has thus been avoided because the owners have participated in their drafting and improvement.

- The documented processes often are viewed as merely a means of retaining certification of some kind. We tried to go a bit further by introducing our intranet. The ease of use and access to continuously updated information are major advantages of using an intranet. These advantages help counteract the fears some staff have regarding dealing with computers. Without this ease of accessing all important company documents with a mouse click from any workplace, our project could not succeed.

The feeling of belonging throughout the company has increased greatly, thanks to the projects mentioned here. The team idea promoted by the empowerment program, and the hard and successful work within the SAT team in particular, was decisive here. Setting up the process-oriented management system gave our employees a common vision of coalescing the individual projects to support a company strategy. In the course of introducing this system, staff from various divisions had to define their work processes together. This improved communications among divisions.

These results are specific consequences of the empowerment project and the introduction of process orientation. As part of the former project, for example, approximately 50 percent of the staff were integrated and trained as SAT members after three years. The hierarchical levels have been cut and, hence, the flow of information improved.

All key processes and associated responsibility profiles have been documented. This is the precondition for the process organization being experienced. If the profiles agree with the processes, process orientation becomes a reality within the company. An owner was nominated for every process, with the task of constantly having that process used by the affected staff and keeping it updated. Thereafter, the major process indices were determined, giving the owner a means of continuously monitoring the efficiency of his or her process.

Although it may be difficult to show that some company successes are directly due to our projects, we can certainly state that the productivity in some teams has visibly improved, even breaking some records, and the number of industrial accidents has been greatly reduced.

In three years and in the course of three projects, we have experienced a radical change in managerial and working methods as well as company culture. In the future, we will rely on a management system characterized by coherence among the empowerment, SAP, and process-orientation projects.

Knowledge Management—Core Competence in Competition

Wolfgang Bernhart

> *Knowledge is the only meaningful resource today.*
> —Peter Drucker

Knowledge is the most important and previously inadequately managed company resource in the innovation race of the new millennium. However, knowledge management is much more than merely the use of new technologies. Instead, it is necessary to manage its five dimensions to promote complete knowledge processes in companies: content, culture, context, process, and infrastructure. In this chapter, the basis of this concept will be explained, and examples taken from the automobile industry will be used to demonstrate how knowledge management initiatives can be put into practice successfully.

Knowledge—The Most Important Resource?

The quote from Peter Drucker will be true tomorrow, even more than it is today or than it has been in the past. From where does this interest come, and why is knowledge management only now beginning to become a top management issue?

The past years have considerably changed the structure of the automobile industry. A number of companies have been taken over or forced to rethink their business system and positioning in the value-added chain. The consolidation is continuing, globalization was and is one of the core challenges in the industry, and all major manufacturers are making efforts to cover as many

---

1 The authors thank Larry Chait, vice president of Arthur D. Little who was responsible for the worldwide internal knowledge management, Friedrich Bock, and many other colleagues for their valuable input into this text.

customer segments as possible. At the same time, it is becoming more difficult to maintain competitive advantages in products and productivity.

How, then, can manufacturers and parts suppliers differentiate themselves from their competitors? The answer is: Through innovation.

The most successful companies are those that replace their products before the competition does this for them, develop new sales and service strategies, introduce new production methods, and adapt optimized processes and methods worldwide. The engine for this innovation is knowledge.

The strategic and economic importance of the factor knowledge is undisputed in the industry. Thus, for example, Ford has been using KM systems for some time now and claims to have saved 245 million DM (approximately $100 million) in development costs from 1996 to 1997 with the aid of its best practice replication project.

Other manufacturers have also started pilot projects in selected fields to define which knowledge is actually of strategic importance, to place a value on knowledge, to balance knowledge so that processes for knowledge management can be defined, to install supporting IT systems, and to see how knowledge management can be anchored within the existing company culture.

This is how the stock market values knowledge:

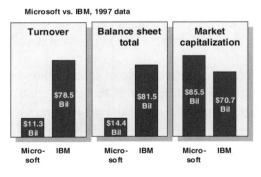

Microsoft vs. IBM, 1997 data

- In 1997, the turnover of IBM was about seven times higher than that of Microsoft. This reflects the strength of IBM whose capital is about 5.7 times higher than that of its much smaller competitor.
- The investors in the stock market appear to ignore these turnover and capital figures, the market valued Microsoft more than 20% higher.

Why? The hidden, unrecognized capital, the knowledge of the organization and its intellectual capital exceed that of IBM.

All of this makes one ask, "Why is knowledge management only now becoming a significant top management theme?"

The reason for the wave of interest lies in a combination of increasingly faster changes and the explosive increase in information—information overload.

Rapid changes are happening everywhere. Never before have so many new vehicles been introduced as will be introduced in the coming few years. New technology concepts such as GPS, telematics, or alternative drive systems are flowing into vehicles. New information and communications technologies are revolutionizing internal processes and cooperation with customers and suppliers. This speed has influenced all organizations. Time-to-market requires conceptual rethinking from "What do we know?" to "Can we use what we know now?"

At the same time, the volume of information has grown enormously. A recent study showed that the volume of data in an average organization doubles every 18 months. In fact, people often are overwhelmed by the sheer volume of information, while it is very difficult to differentiate the important from the unimportant.

The ability of a company to perform in the future will depend increasingly on the ability to convert data and information into knowledge (i.e., on the ability of the entire organization to learn). Knowledge management is a concept to identify and secure the gigantic store of knowledge which is in the organization and its business partners, suppliers, and customers, so that what is known is also what is used.

Let us recapitulate the situation as it stands and review the challenges described in the other chapters of this book.

In an environment of increasingly rapid change, information is available nearly everywhere in the world which:

- Offers opportunities and risks for the long-honored basis of competition

- Makes new forms of knowledge-based competition based on the intellectual capital of a company increasingly possible and necessary

197

- Will in turn accelerate the pace of change and further increase the necessity of professional management of knowledge

As Ken Barker, vice president of the GM Research and Development Centers, tellingly stated, "Speed to knowledge is the new basis of competition." Knowledge appears as a core resource next to capital and labor.

Companies have always tried to use the knowledge they possess, and they have (even if only implicitly) always managed it. Every manufacturer and supplier can know so much today and use this knowledge so much faster that a clear focus on knowledge management becomes necessary.

But what is the situation like today?

Various surveys have shown: Knowledge that is not adequately transferred is not available when it is needed the most, critical knowledge is only in the heads of the employees, and few systematized processes and measured variables are available to ensure that knowledge is shared (Fig. 1).

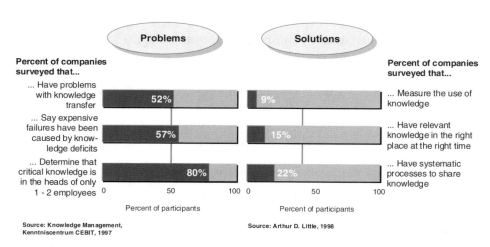

Figure 1   Knowledge—current problems and the state of knowledge management.

A benchmarking study by the American Productivity and Quality Council also determined that only 16 percent of companies measure the value of their intellectual capital and the knowledge of their organizations.

Hardly any company manages knowledge with the intensity and efficiency with which it manages the other factors of production, capital, and labor. Why? First, knowledge is often viewed as an abstract concept that may have only little to do with the daily business, especially in the automobile industry which has a strong technical bias because it is dominated by practical people. Furthermore, it is difficult to determine where valuable knowledge is; who is responsible for it; and how it can be budgeted, valued, and written off. It is difficult to measure, count, or place a monetary value on knowledge. One of the more important factors of production of the future—knowledge—is not adequately managed.

Knowledge Management Is More than Merely Databases, Notes, and an Intranet

The starting point for many knowledge management projects and initiatives often is the availability of new technical-organizational solutions such as workflow management, data warehousing, MIS (Management Information Systems), or an intranet. The hope that a more powerful IT system can completely solve the problems of recording, storing, and distributing knowledge often, however, proves to be illusory. Information systems form only the infrastructure. They do not create knowledge; they merely transport it. The management of knowledge, therefore, does not mean the installation of expensive networks and the release of all information for complete communication.

Case Study: Technology Alone Is Not Enough

A new product development process has been being implemented for the last four years at Ford at great expense. This process is available to all engineers in the company-owned intranet as online documentation and should be available in all development departments by the year 2000. This should also include the suppliers. One of the most important steps in this process is the updating of the knowledge basis in which a complete project is analyzed with respect to "lessons learned."

> The results of this criticism of the maneuver then wander into the "corporate memory" and should be available to all employees via the intranet. According to statements by the development executives, much work remains to be done here because the intranet is "not yet being very actively used."
>
> Source: *Automobilproduktion, Sonderheft Qualität,* July 1997.

Instead, our project experience at Arthur D. Little shows that three key factors are critical for every knowledge management initiative:

- A solid basis in the company
- A multidimensional focus
- A consistent, clear, and communicated plan

Here, a solid basis means that a clear vision of knowledge management exists and that the company supports this vision.

This vision should be based on the goals and strategies of the company or division. Company goals and the demands of business must be known. Clear ideas of how knowledge can help here should exist or be developed.

Furthermore, the company must support this vision. Not only is consensus necessary, but clear promotion on the part of the top management must occur. For this to happen, it is necessary to develop a clear, common picture of the future that the company wants to achieve. This picture must be contrasted by an equally clear picture of the current reality. In further workshops, a concrete action plan is worked out on how to achieve the common goals that were defined.

The second factor is to manage knowledge as a multidimensional process, to promote complete knowledge processes in the company, and to target performance improvements specifically. Knowledge management can be seen as the ability of an organization to actively drive and exploit its know-how in order to increase the intellectual capital and company earnings. It covers five dimensions: content, context, culture, process, and tools/infrastructure (Fig. 2).

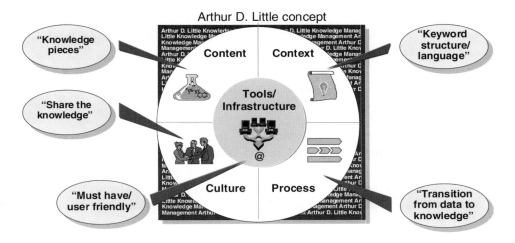

Figure 2   Knowledge management as a multidimensional process.

Typical pitfalls result from overemphasizing or neglecting some dimensions of successful knowledge management and from insufficient management support:

1. *Content*—Too much information is considered important. It becomes a major effort to capture all of the content, people become frustrated, and the benefit is questionable.

2. *Culture*—Cultural issues are neglected; knowledge is not shared. This leads to a high risk of project failure.

3. *Context*—The contextual environment is not properly defined; thus, retrieval of the information is frustrating or fails to deliver.

4. *Process*—The process is incomplete and does not address the needs of the different groups that provide, access, and share knowledge.

5. *Infrastructure/Tools*—People become carried away by features of IT tools; IT dominates the approach. After some initial excitement, people can become frustrated.

If management does not pay enough attention and wants a cheap solution, the effort is considered low priority by participants and the results remain unsatisfactory.

Content—Placing the Focus on Strategically Relevant Knowledge

The question "What do we have to know?" should always be answered based on the strategic importance and uniqueness of the knowledge required. This question concerns not only technologies or expert knowledge that is used in production processes, but extends much further to knowledge of markets, customers, suppliers, etc.—that is, from all fields of the business.

Daimler-Benz, for example, has made the decision to learn from the projects for the A Class, the M Class, and the SMART in its SOKRATES project. To do this, individual processes and fields of learning were prioritized to supply knowledge useful in the classic product lines such as the C, E, and S Classes. This includes newly developed capabilities—for example, how to address new target groups, what should be considered when opening new production sites, or how to work with highly integrated suppliers.

Too many companies select the opposite approach: They collect every kind of knowledge they can think of and place it in a network in the hope that someone will be able to find the knowledge they need. The result is necessarily a "data graveyard" with huge quantities of redundant or unnecessary information. Multifunctional teams that are looking for useful knowledge are forced to analyze large quantities of data simply to be able to identify the information required and to derive the important knowledge from it. They have to know this even if they only want to know if their project is still within accepted norms or if threatening problems already exist.

According to our experience, it has proven to be more useful to first evaluate the individual fields of knowledge and then work out a knowledge management strategy for these fields.

Using criteria such as importance for the core business, contribution to knowledge of core processes of the company, expandability, uniqueness, risk, and urgency, a portfolio of standard strategies can be defined for management of the "intellectual capital" (Fig. 3).

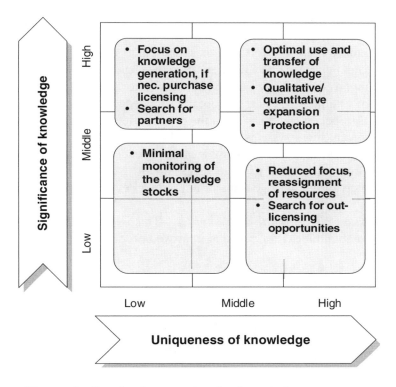

Figure 3   Standard strategies for knowledge management.

The result should be specific goals and actions which are defined for each field of knowledge—for example, to balance deficits or to license knowledge that is strategically less relevant to third parties. This includes a description of the depth of the expertise as well as specific acquisition strategies for every single case where knowledge leadership is desired and where it is merely adequate to be a follower.

Case Study:
Technology Licensing of the GM R&D Center

Four important channels of knowledge acquisition can be differentiated:

- *Knowledge from other companies*—In addition to benchmarking activities, alliances, mergers, and acquisitions are especially good ways to quickly build the knowledge capital of a company and to immediately convert it into shareholder value. The merger of Daimler-Benz and Chrysler offers the chance for those companies involved to use new sources of knowledge. Thus, the Chrysler part of DaimlerChrysler can obtain knowledge on market access to Europe, on technologies in the product field, and effective quality management systems. The Daimler part can use Chrysler knowledge on supply chain management to reduce its cost of materials. Both parts now use the *Engineering Book of Knowledge* to increase knowledge transfer in product development.

- *Knowledge from the stakeholder*—This is a cost-effective means to obtain ideas for new and improved products and services. The

Active marketing of non-core competencies in the Internet.

early inclusion of customers in the product development process can provide valuable knowledge about the needs of the target group. Thus, for example, Volkswagen placed a picture of the New Beetle on the Internet even before the market introduction in the United States so that comments from potential customers could be gathered and considered in the development of the details.

- *Knowledge pieces*—Examples include software, licenses, analyses, and reports.

- *Experts*—Companies can either recruit specialists externally, hire them away from others, or hire them as consultants. The change of Lopéz to Volkswagen and the successes subsequently recorded in supply chain management and production optimization show the potential that the purchase of external know-how can have. Management consultants are being hired more often to transfer specialized knowledge to the company's own employees, and less to prepare analyses and audits.

Case Study:
Learning in Alliances—Using the Knowledge of Other Companies

Honda was the first Japanese automobile company to jointly produce a vehicle with a European company when it entered into its alliance with Rover. At that time, Rover had a history as a producer of good luxury vehicles but also had considerable problems with quality and productivity. Honda produced excellent small cars and had very efficient production methods. Rover needed money, and Honda needed access to the European markets. Therefore, Honda invested in Rover and began production in England. In the course of this alliance, Honda learned very well and jointly developed the Legend sedan with Rover, which then was successfully marketed in the United States as the Acura. This made Honda the first Japanese producer to move into the high-class market segment in the United States, even before Toyota with the Lexus and Nissan with the Infinity. Honda's market entry was successful although, in contrast to Toyota and Nissan, it had had no previous experience with the production of such vehicles.

Behavior and Company Culture—The Basis of Knowledge Management

The second dimension is culture. To answer the question of how knowledge exchange can be promoted, first we need to differentiate between two types of knowledge: (1) explicit knowledge, and (2) tacit knowledge—that is, knowledge that is not expressed or is implicit.

Explicit knowledge generally can be easily codified in handbooks, process descriptions, and databases (e.g., procedures, formulas, rules, and instructions). This knowledge remains in the company even when employees leave the company. However, another type of knowledge is the so-called tacit knowledge. This is know-how, experience, and informal knowledge that is not documented and that experienced employees and managers bring to their work, and it is usually the basis of any advantage over the competition. This knowledge is permanently in danger of being lost due to the loss of employees.

How much such undocumented know-how disappears through the loss and exchange of employees can be comprehended when we examine the development of the number of employees in the German automotive parts suppliers. Between 1990 and 1994, 20 percent of the employees were eliminated. If we also include the normal fluctuation due to people quitting and retiring, we get the idea that many companies in the industry lost or exchanged more that half of their employees—and with them their rich treasure of know-how and knowledge.

The risk of losing knowledge makes it necessary to identify tacit knowledge in the companies earlier and to make it available to the organization. This is one of the operative core tasks of knowledge management.

How can this be done? How are experiences from individual activities adapted to new situations? How can best practices be copied? In other words, how do the processes of organizational learning function?

The transfer of existing organizational knowledge is based on the four basic learning processes of adaptation and replication (Fig. 4).

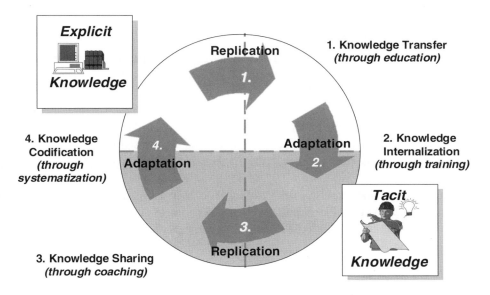

Figure 4   The four basic processes for the transfer of existing organizational knowledge.

First is the transfer of explicit knowledge, e.g., when reading a benchmarking study or during participation in a congress on the use of certain new technologies. The basis for the spread of explicit knowledge is books, databases, microfilms, and IT systems. For this knowledge to be used, it must be adapted, either through individual study or through training. This enables explicit knowledge to become individual abilities. This second critical step is the essential part of individual, team, or organizational training. Only through use are "bare" theories internalized. Some abilities (e.g., convincing a customer of the advantages of a new car and successfully concluding the sales process) are more difficult to describe in words or to treat with exercises. The best way to transfer this non-explicit knowledge is through a coach or through the work in teams in which work toward a solution is joint. At the latest, this third learning process of knowledge sharing through coaching is the point where most companies stop. However, the systematization of knowledge—for example, through writing down the knowledge gained in a vehicle project—creates the basis for an efficient transfer through media.

Furthermore, there are two additional important learning processes to create new knowledge: On the one hand, the continuous improvement of methods and procedures, and on the other hand, the rather rapid learning though innovation processes.

Most companies fail at this point to make discrete, hidden knowledge of individuals available to the whole organization. A current study lists the finding of new ways to jointly use this tacit knowledge as the most important task of knowledge management other than the organization of the existing knowledge.

To successfully anchor this fourth learning process in companies, it is necessary to understand the behavioral patterns that determine the division of individual know-how because this individual knowledge makes an employee useful to the company (Table 1).

TABLE 1
THE BEHAVIORAL ASPECT OF TACIT KNOWLEDGE

Reality in Companies	
How is individual knowledge used?	**What are the implications?**
Tacit Knowledge...	
...frequently includes tips and tricks to accomplish the daily work faster or more efficiently than others.	...is used, but not openly displayed; to reveal it is the same as "giving it away."
...is used to work outside the formal system.	...is actively hidden.
...is often used for self-portrayal.	...is something similar to property.
...is an instrument of power in many companies.	...to hoard it means to have power, or at least protection (e.g., from being fired)

The reduction in the number of personnel that has taken place in the last few years, especially in middle management, has frequently made the "survivors" even more distrustful when the question concerns revealing their individual knowledge to third parties. They do everything to protect their valuable trade goods. In addition to these barriers, which make the transfer of individual knowledge more difficult, the use of knowledge by others is made more difficult by the "not-invented-here syndrome." In nearly every project, we encounter people with doubts who make every effort to prove that others' approaches to solutions are not applicable in this special case.

A lack of willingness to share knowledge or to accept the knowledge of others is often the reason that factories with identical technologies frequently operate at different capacities. A lack of willingness makes it difficult to transfer good approaches—best practices—from one location to another.

Various studies have shown that a culture oriented toward the exchange of knowledge is the most important criterion for successful knowledge management. Astonishingly, this aspect is typically the one most neglected. The result of this inadequate consideration is that cultural problems often compose more than 50 percent of a project and create tremendous complexity. In a survey recently conducted by Arthur D. Little among top management in German companies, more than 80 percent of the participants said they see the sharing and use of knowledge as a cultural problem in their companies.

This does not mean that every company initiative should try to change the culture, but it does at least mean that a change in employee behavior must occur.

If one desires real and lasting changes in behaviors which are due to one's own motivation rather than pressure, it is necessary to uncover the cultural reality. To do this, the patterns of the unwritten rules that govern the daily business and reflect the hopes and desires of those involved must be analyzed. The management must understand the mental models that are the cause of fear, rejection of passing knowledge to others, or accepting it from others. Only then can the external framework—the written rules—be changed (Fig. 5).

The methodology of the unwritten rules developed by Arthur D. Little has proven effective in uncovering these behaviors. This analysis takes three to four weeks and is based on a large number of interviews which typically are conducted with the middle management. The objects of these conversations are the desired and undesired side effects of written and unwritten rules with reference to the exchange of knowledge.

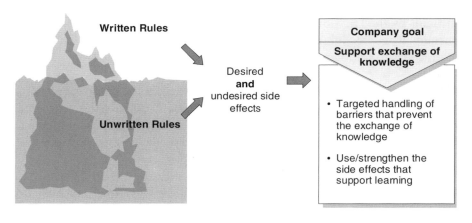

Figure 5   Unwritten rules create side effects against which targeted actions are necessary to support the exchange of knowledge.

In the next step, the observations made in the interviews are structured into three groups: motivators, enablers, and triggers.

Motivators are attitudes, hopes, and fears that are important to the employees—that which motivates them. What do the employees expect from their professions? What conditions do they want to avoid? Why do they go to the plant on Monday mornings? These attracting and repelling "magnets" listed by those interviewed are then summarized into groups in the next step. Typical motivators are, for example, the freedom of the developer to self-actualization, the pride of working in a world-class company, the opportunity to make a career, or the fear of losing the job. Motivators explain what is really important to individual employees. For this reason, expressions such as customer orientation usually do not appear, even when the employee is informed innumerable times of the importance of these values. Typically, three to five motivators form the core of the culture of a company, and one should not try to change them.

Closely linked to the question "What is important?" is the question "Who is important?" These are the enablers who make it possible for employees to achieve what is important to them. Who can get you the hoped-for reward for good performance or see that you do not have to work on an uninteresting project? Typically, supervisors are listed here, but other persons or systems exercise power in a company. The interviews are designed to uncover the real power structure in a company—the "unwritten organization." Frequently numbered among these are, in addition to the line functions, other persons (e.g., the assistant to the manager or the Works' Council).

Triggers are the proximate causes that enable the individual to achieve what he or she wants—the circumstances that guide an enabler (e.g., the real reason why a supervisor suggests a bonus, promotes someone, or warns some-one). Triggers also usually contain all the formal and informal evaluation systems in the company.

The concrete situation in the company can be described using these motivators, enablers, and triggers as well as using the written and experienced (unwritten) rules of the game. These lead to undesired side effects which must be over-come to successfully practice the exchange of knowledge and to support the desired side effects that can be used to support organizational learning.

Case Study:
Cultural Barriers to the Transfer of Knowledge (1)

Based on a fictitious example, that of Motor Inc., which has been derived from various experiences Arthur D. Little has had in projects, the functioning of the written and unwritten rules, motivators, enablers, and triggers becomes clear.

The main motivator to work for Motor Inc. is to have a career in a world-class company. How is this motivator influenced by the written rules of the game? The first rule was: "Managers of Motor Inc. are recruited internally by preference." The unwritten rule that lies behind this is: "Other companies are worse; don't get the nest dirty."

What about enablers, the factors that exercise power? A second writ-ten rule is: "The best managers are promoted the fastest"—by their line bosses. A corresponding unwritten rule here is: "Show that you are the best." The other side of the coin is: "Avoid being associated with failures if you want to be promoted." If someone suppresses his ego and shares his knowledge, and speaks of avoidable failures, he might be considered to be running down the company and is perhaps quite right when he fears that another who has put himself into the right

211

position will be promoted instead of him because most company internal competition is done using knowledge.

Regardless of whether we support or reject these behaviors, they are understandable and even logical. Everyone who works under these conditions will behave similarly.

What role, then, do the triggers play? The third written rule is: "Managers are responsible for their turnover and their center results." This is intended to ensure that the management acts economically and with an orientation toward the customer. However, if we take a look at the unwritten rules, they are as logical and predictable as the others.

The most important rule is: "Check your turnover; it goes to the cheapest plant." Although the board may be speaking of the learning organization and change management, as soon as the phone rings, the priorities are clear. There is no reward for having considerably increased performance in other fields. The day only has 24 hours, and those affected know what is most important and what is not so important to reach their own goals in the mess of motivators, enablers, and triggers.

Written and unwritten rules are, in and of themselves, neither good nor bad. The question is: How do the unwritten rules influence the culture of open exchange of knowledge? With rules such as "Avoid being associated with failures," it is difficult to communicate avoidable errors from projects, to learn from them, and to avoid them in the future.

The unwritten rules are the missing link in the chain to uncovering cultural problems early in knowledge management. It is not enough, however, to know these rules. Instead, it is important to understand how they are linked to the tip of the iceberg—the written rules above the surface of the water, the values experienced in the company that reward the non-sharing usage of knowledge. Employees must be allowed to learn, and evaluation systems and measured variables must support this process. To remain with our metaphor of the iceberg, it is not enough to simply view the iceberg. Instead, the entire current, the interchanges, must be considered if undesirable side effects are not to destroy other fields when individual rules or evaluation systems are changed. The basis for this is "systems thinking," a method of organizational learning which our colleagues from our subsidiary Innovation Associates helped develop.

Case Study:
Cultural Barriers to the Transfer of Knowledge (2)

What can Motor Inc. do now to clear away obstacles to the best possible use of knowledge? In this process, the desired effects (namely, of offering employees the most attractive opportunities in the company, to create a climate oriented toward performance, and to promote customer and results orientation) must not be reduced.

Different approaches are possible which must be evaluated in the actual context of the company: The managers and employees of Motor Inc. can be measured using many different variables, among others on their contribution to the increase of certain "intellectual assets."

This can be done with approaches such as the balanced scorecard. Motor Inc. could establish a knowledge market in which individual centers offer specific know-how. Or it can, perhaps, get rid of Rule 1 (internal recruiting) and evaluate internal and external applicants using the same standards.

Context—The Framework for Easy Retrieval of Corporate Knowledge

The third dimension of knowledge management—the context—is essential for a successful retrieval of stored knowledge.

Everybody knows how frustrating surfing the Internet can be. You obtain an enormous number of answers to a specific question, but unfortunately these answers do not answer your specific needs. The reason for that is an improperly defined context of the knowledge piece.

Consider a study relating to the market and the competitive environment for engines in Japan which your marketing department might have prepared. It covers a forecast on the market size and demand for common rail technology, the strengths and weaknesses of your competitors and their products in

Japan, and a chapter on future legislation related to emissions you might expect in Japan. In addition, you might have another 10 studies on engines, 5 on the Japanese market, and another 32 on legislation covering all aspects of the automotive industry.

If you are seeking input data to prepare a strategy to enter the Asian market with a new engine technology, you want to obtain immediate access to exactly this study. You do not want to be bothered with the other 57 studies mentioned in your knowledge management system, which all add only a little or no value to your task.

The key for that is the context. To find the best-suited knowledge piece, you must be able to use a multidimensional, hierarchical thesaurus. Such a thesaurus must deliver you a link to the study if you ask "What do we have on engines in Asia?" or if you ask "What do we know about the strengths of Nissan Diesel?" as well as if you ask "What do we know about the demand for common rail technology?"

The context must be defined with respect to the anticipated questions the potential users might have. Therefore, you should take a close look inside the processes to be supported.

The Process of Knowledge Management

The fourth dimension of knowledge management is the process. Included among these are activities, roles, and responsibilities (Fig. 6).

Processes exist at different levels. First, there is the process of knowledge management, how knowledge is generated, how it is evaluated, how it is stored, and how it is made available. The expression "knowledge management process," however, also refers to existing processes in the company. In our experience, it is impossible to take a process such as the one depicted and include it as a whole in the existing business processes.

To manage the process dimension of knowledge management, it is better first to design the ideal knowledge process for the company in question, then to analyze the existing processes and to work out how elements of the knowledge management process can be integrated into the daily work.

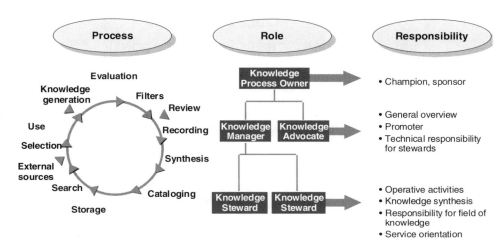

Figure 6   Example of activities, roles, and responsibilities in the process of knowledge management.

Furthermore, the process dimension also contains roles and responsibilities. The description of these roles requires the analysis of the current work contents, roles, and responsibilities. Building from such an assessment, either the existing jobs can be redefined and/or new jobs can be created which include these roles. Although some companies, especially from the IT industry, create completely new jobs, we believe it is more appropriate for automobile companies and their suppliers to define new roles that are performed in parallel to previous tasks.

Third, the process dimension must answer questions of control—responsibility of the management, reporting paths, etc. Table 2 lists some frequently asked questions and their answers which we have derived from our multi-industry study of successful knowledge management initiatives.

Infrastructure and Technology— Necessary, But Not Enough

The fifth dimension of knowledge management is the infrastructure. Numbered among these are aspects of the automation of knowledge management. However, IT systems are only part of the solution. They must be supplemented with other elements such as education, training, coaching, and the general support of those involved in the process.

TABLE 2

BEST PRACTICE IN THE ROLE DISTRIBUTION OF KNOWLEDGE MANAGEMENT

Frequently asked questions and their answers on responsibilities in knowledge management	
What responsibility does the board of directors, the board of management, and senior management have?	Each identifies with the knowledge management initiative, a top management member is an "active champion."
To whom should the knowledge management initiative report?	The initiative should report to the top management of the company, to the chairman of the board, or to the president. Reporting through a functional department (IT or personnel) can, if not properly managed, reduce the importance of the subject and dilute the focus.
Who should drive forward the initiative?	The requirement is the understanding of the business, respect, and influence within the company.
What are the roles and responsibilities of all the other employees?	The concrete responsibility is to be defined depending on the specifics of the company in question.

Although the available technology is one of the most important driving forces for knowledge management, it cannot do the work by itself. However, it can help to store, distribute, localize, and evaluate the different aspects of knowledge.

Even if technology is developing rapidly, it can be stated that powerful retrieval software combined with an intranet architecture fulfills the specifications for a global knowledge management system in an ideal way (Fig. 7).

Case Study:
Use of the Latest Technologies and Inclusion of the Existing Information Systems in the BMW Knowledge Marketplace

The goal of the implementation of the knowledge marketplace in the Research and Engineering Center in Munich was to create a pool of knowledge that was easy to use in order to accelerate the development of vehicles. The system uses existing databases from the various departments and uses the networked desktop computers with browser

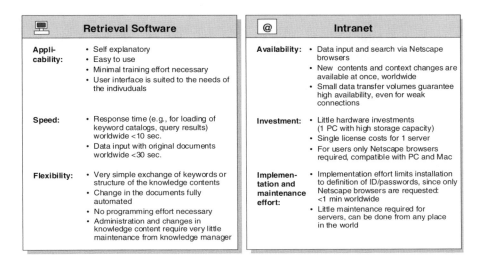

Retrieval Software	
Appli-cability:	• Self explanatory • Easy to use • Minimal training effort necessary • User interface is suited to the needs of the indivuduals
Speed:	• Response time (e.g., for loading of keyword catalogs, query results) worldwide <10 sec. • Data input with original documents worldwide <30 sec.
Flexibility:	• Very simple exchange of keywords or structure of the knowledge contents • Change in the documents fully automated • No programming effort necessary • Administration and changes in knowledge content require very little maintenance from knowledge manager

@ Intranet	
Availability:	• Data input and search via Netscape browsers • New contents and context changes are available at once, worldwide • Small data transfer volumes guarantee high availability, even for weak connections
Investment:	• Little hardware investments (1 PC with high storage capacity) • Single license costs for 1 server • For users only Netscape browsers required, compatible with PC and Mac
Implemen-tation and maintenance effort:	• Implementation effort limits installation to definition of ID/passwords, since only Netscape browsers are requested: <1 min worldwide • Little maintenance required for servers, can be done from any place in the world

Figure 7 Comparison of different IT solutions for knowledge management.

software as the access system. Only the meta-model, which is placed in a "knowledge repository" and which, similarly to a roadmap, records the source and location of the knowledge, is new.

With the aid of new technologies and tools such as an intranet, Java, and search engines, the distributed information can be found quickly. Among these are the BMW intranet, all documents on processes and projects, and various databases including external sources. Using "dynamic yellow pages," employees can be found who are linked with specific key words and competencies (skill mining)—sort of a "who's who" to find a contact person quickly.

Source: *Computerwoche*, October 4, 1998.

Technology is critical for knowledge management, but technology is not more than 20 percent of the solution. The greatest challenge is bringing people together so that they can share knowledge directly with each other.

Example:
Tech Clubs and the *Engineering Book of Knowledge* (EBOK) in DaimlerChrysler's Auburn Hill Tech Center

The EBOK can be seen as the genesis of Chrysler's car-making bible, a LotusNotes/Netscape browser-based repository that uses grapeVine Technologies Taxonomy and NewsEdges' new services. It consists of 3,800 chapters, of which approximately 55 percent were completed by early 1999, and is part of the official design review process of the company.

The Tech Clubs (there are seven main clubs which cover body, chassis, advanced engineering, electronics, interior, powertrain, and vehicle development, as well as another 120 Sub Tech Clubs) are regular social gatherings which are crucial to sharing knowledge and mentoring while also providing a formal legislative body to govern the EBOK. In the biweekly gatherings, Tech Coordinators assign authors for EBOK chapters and review and edit submissions until they are accepted as Chrysler's technical and process memory.

Source: *Knowledge Management*, May 1999.

The EBOK and the Tech Clubs currently are introduced in the Daimler part of DaimlerChrysler as well.

How Can Implementation Be Done in Practice?

A solid basis in the company and the five dimensions of knowledge management discussed—content, culture, context, process, and infrastructure—are only two of three factors that make a knowledge management initiative successful. Above and beyond that, a clear and communicated plan for implementation is necessary.

We believe that there is not only one best way to successfully implement knowledge management. However, every project plan must answer several questions:

- With which elements should one start?
- How can a culture of knowledge exchange be developed?

- How can employees be motivated to participate?

- How should the new processes be defined and implemented?

- How should a thesaurus appear?

- Should the new processes be supported technically? If yes, what and how?

- How should the plan and the expectations of the management be communicated?

The specific characteristics depend on the company, its culture, the specific requirements, and priorities; however, all five dimensions must be approached simultaneously.

We have a series of lessons learned that have been gathered from projects in various industries, and tips and tricks at the end of this chapter, as follows:

- Link the knowledge management initiative directly with the company strategy and other important projects and initiatives in the company.

- Commitment is important. The top management must stand behind all efforts toward knowledge management as a group.

- There is no standard approach. Every methodology must be adapted to the specific conditions within the company.

- Be demanding. What used to take weeks or months should now take hours or days.

- Be pragmatic. Start with a few small projects that can be implemented quickly and that achieve rapid successes.

- Define clear responsibilities and roles.

- Do not underestimate the efforts necessary to bring proper processes and a well-defined context into place.

- Do not focus on technology as the solution. It cannot be, and the initiative will fail.

- Use IT systems as the powerful tools they are, but be ready for the dizzying tempo of release-change frequencies.

- Be flexible. Knowledge management is a learning process that yields greater profit when it is adapted to the changed circumstances and can grow over time.

Literature

Hastbacka, M., and McCarthy, K., "Technology Licensing: A Strategy for Creating Value," *Prism* 2/98, Cambridge, MA.

Jonash, R., and Sommerlatte, T., The Innovation Premium, 1999.

Maira, A., and Scott-Morgan, P., *The Accelerating Organization*, McGraw-Hill, New York, 1997.

Probst, G., "Practical Knowledge Management: A Model that Works," *Prism* 2/98, Cambridge, MA.

Scott-Morgan, P., *The Unwritten Rules of the Game*, New York, 1994.

High-Performance Full-Service Car Management

Gerrit Seidel, Stefan Richter

> *You can never overtake someone*
> *when you're walking in his footsteps.*
> —François Truffaut

The upward trend in the leasing of movable property remains unchanged. In the last two years, the average growth has been more than 10 percent per year. A clear growth trend for the coming years is emerging as well. The expansion of the service and product range toward a concept of mobility and strengthened global engagement in the international markets fits well with the further potential for expansion and earnings.

At the same time, e-commerce is revolutionizing full-service car and fleet management, and the intensity of competition is increasing due to strong international banks, financial captives, and independent service companies. In demand are service and operate leasing, complete mobility solutions, equipment expertise, and remarketing capability in a web-based Internet environment. The market changes rapidly—time is ticking away.

Using the Changes in the Leasing Market

The international markets are ahead of the German market. According to current estimates, approximately 50 percent of all investments in movable equipment in Europe are financed out of cash flow, and approximately 50 percent are financed through borrowing. At least half of this will cover leasing. Although the importance of leasing movable property has increased as a financial instrument in Germany in the last few years and approximately 20 percent of all investments in equipment were leased in 1998, Germany continues to lag behind in international comparisons. Especially when compared to the United States (31 percent) and Great Britain (29 percent), considerable growth potential exists (Fig. 1).

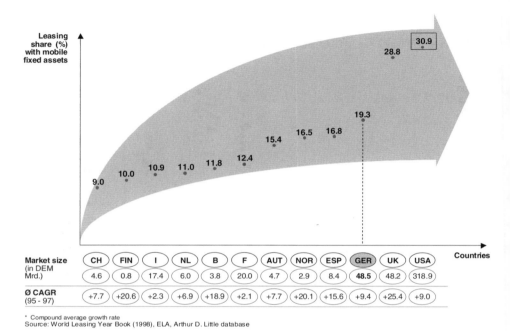

Figure 1   Proportion of leasing for investments in movable equipment.

In addition to the differing financial and tax conditions, the differences are due mainly to highly profitable and innovative leasing and financial products in the commercial and private sectors which contain comprehensive service components and assumption of risk by the lessor. A corresponding focus on these challenges by German firms in this sector therefore seems appropriate.

Forced Competition

The cards in the leasing market are being reshuffled. The competition in the industry is increasing continuously. Financial captives such as Ford Credit Corporation, GMAC Financial Services, or DaimlerChrysler Financial Services are handling their business, which is tied to their manufacturing parents and increasingly their third-party business as well, professionally. American and Anglo-Saxon companies such as PHH Vehicle Management and Associates Fleet Services or the Lombard Group work internationally with their operate leasing subsidiaries in the automotive sector. The Dutch credit institutes are setting up their leasing companies internationally (Leaseplan/ABN Amro, Athlon Group) and are increasingly using synergies with the commercial and investment banking activities of their parents. In Germany, this is becoming increasingly clear—on the one hand, from the consolidation of the leasing activities, and, on the other hand, through the efforts of some suppliers to acquire new market segments.

Trend Toward Full-Service Car Management

Vehicles now have a proportion of more than 60 percent of the total leasing of movable property in Germany, in comparison to the United States, a heavyweight. However, market estimates show that in 1997 in Germany, only approximately 245,000 full-service leasing contracts and about 62,000 so-called management contracts, which are not leased but transferred to external service companies, were concluded. The full-service policies in force were equivalent to a market share as a proportion of the total market of vehicles used commercially of approximately 15 percent: in international comparisons to Great Britain at 43 percent, France at 23 percent, and Benelux with 22 percent, a rather modest figure. If one examines the structure of full-service leasing in the field of company vehicle parks, the picture appears even more extreme: only approximately 18 percent of the commercially leased vehicles in German companies are part of a full-service contract, compared to 90 percent in England and 75 percent in France.

The German market for "car fleet management" therefore has been opened at most by 25 percent. The outsourcing efforts of the company customers and fleet managers are causing or strengthening this trend. In Germany, a need exists to catch up in the full-service sector, which will mean doubling the totals in the next three to five years. Companies such as debis Car Fleet Management, FMD Flottenmanagement Deutschland, or DEKRA/VR Leasing Fleetservices expect growth potentials of 20 to 50 percent in the coming years. Penetration rates, which were at 17 percent in 1997, will increase to nearly 30 percent in the next millennium (Fig. 2).

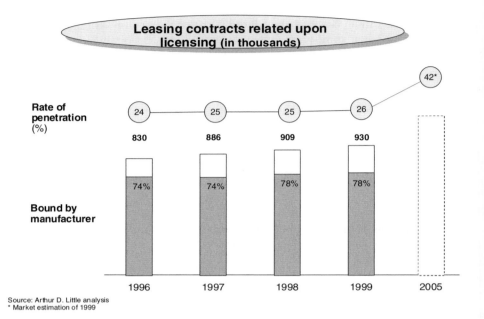

Leasing contracts related upon licensing (in thousands)

Rate of penetration (%)

| 24 | 25 | 25 | 26 | 42* |

| 830 | 886 | 909 | 930 |

| 74% | 74% | 78% | 78% |

Bound by manufacturer

| 1996 | 1997 | 1998 | 1999 | 2005 |

Source: Arthur D. Little analysis
* Market estimation of 1999

Figure 2 Narrow growth carried by long-term rental.

A giant step forward can also be seen in the long-term rental market segment. Its proportion of the total market for car rentals in Germany will increase from 4 percent today (1997) to approximately 12 percent by the year 2004. This growth trend remains unbroken for Europe as well. There, the numbers in the full-service sector will increase from approximately 2.8 million vehicles to 3.9 million in 2001.

Narrow Market and International Players

In accordance with this trend, it is not surprising that most leasing companies have set themselves very high goals and still want to achieve double-digit growth rates. However, it is uncertain whether "American/European full-service leasing conditions" will apply to all markets in the next three to five years.

This is true first, because the markets are only partially comparable, and second, there is an increasing tendency toward destructive competition. Although the market can display considerable growth potential, the number of full-service providers has increased rapidly—yes, even faster than the market itself has grown. In addition to the financially strong captives of the automobile manufacturers which led this market to maturity, plenty of new entrants now have appeared on the market: full-service lessors, fleet managers, mineral oil companies, gas station card organizations, insurers, claims adjusters, logistical partners, software houses, and tire makers. Nearly every organization and every company that feels competent in the automobile business or has enough cars and trucks in stock to enter the market as a service company for third parties wants to participate. In the course of the globalization of markets, international companies such as PHH Corporation or Lex Vehicle Leasing are joining the market, sometimes with their own offices but often with network partners that are found throughout the full-service landscape (Fig. 3).

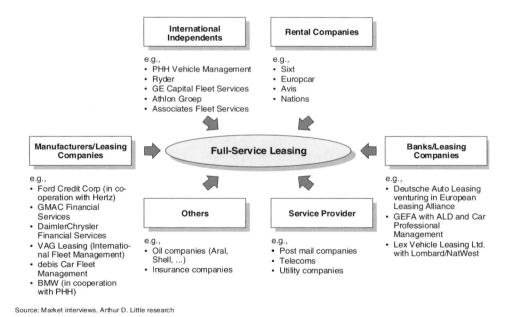

Figure 3 The "run" on the full-service market has begun.

In the long term, four groups of suppliers will control the market:

1. The auto leasing companies, which are independent of the car makers and the auto banks

2. The full-service leasing companies, which are independent of the car makers with a banking background

3. The leasing companies of the large car rental companies (as conglomerates)

4. The service providers for car fleet management (including car consulting and software providers)

The experiences that they will have or have already had on their course of expansion are that market entry is expensive, the margins in the standard business are too low, full service is personnel-intensive, and the IT demands are complex.

Customer-Oriented Product Building Blocks

"Money is a commodity." The classic financing of the vehicle is no longer suitable as a differentiation factor, and as a "money over money business" delivers only modest profitability. The service management, therefore, must and will develop further. In addition to the pure finance and handling activities, customer service and repair services, coordination, and controlling are numbered among the core tasks in full-service car management. This creates a new demand profile for the service provider and a differentiated product profile for fleet management service: The service providers of tomorrow will have to be fast, flexible, reliable, customer-oriented, networked, and cooperative.

Making total mobility available will be the characteristic for differentiation. This includes the transfer of use of the vehicles and their integration into a total mobility concept. Exceeding the commercial vehicle business—*à la* Mercedes-Benz CharterWay or Ryder System—service contracts, short-term rental models, interim vehicles, road haulage, remuneration after value added to the customer, and e-business applications will increase (Fig. 4).

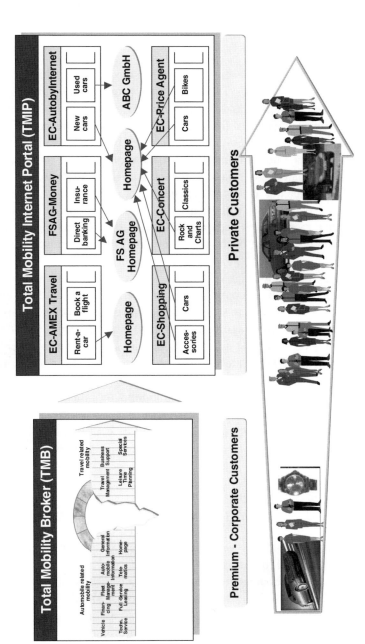

Figure 4   Total mobility broker concept.

Mastering the Challenges in Full-Service Car Management

To do this, it will be necessary to build a close relationship with the manufacturer and the product. The full-service provider must manage the four-way relationship among the manufacturer, network partners, customer, and himself. The dominance of the leasing companies that are tied to a manufacturer in the field of automobile leasing cannot be overlooked here. This is little wonder when one examines the constellation in which these companies act in the marketplace. As financial captives of the manufacturer, these providers profit from easier access to the end customer via the dealer networks. Comprehensive databases offer nearly inexhaustible sources of potential contacts and customer data. Furthermore, knowledge of existing, as well as future, products on the part of the parent companies is an added plus.

Beyond that, knowledge of the industry is of decisive importance, especially when it concerns a "complete solution" for the customer. Among these are numbered, in addition to the classic administrative work for registration, taxes, and insurance (management services), maintenance, repair, and claims estimates/adjustments (technical services); leasing and rental (financial services); and other value added services, for example, in the form of consulting on acquisition or vehicle exchange, the creation of logistics or communications concepts—all under the aspect of individual mobility. Here, knowledge of the underlying base markets and the mobility features are of prime importance. The automobile as a mobility object and its continuing value become the key factors for success.

Complete Service for the Customer— Developing Modular Products

If the focus yesterday was financial leasing, today it is full-service leasing. Tomorrow it will be called mobility guaranty. The day after tomorrow, people will be talking about integrated mobility concepts that go far beyond the car. For complete care of the customer, that customer should be served in all sectors along the value added chain. Auto leasing and auto rental will converge, and multiple-use concepts such as car-sharing or car-pooling will become the primary carriers for integrated traffic concepts. The travel agent of the future could be a palmtop with a global positioning system (GPS) and an Internet connection, which can immediately determine the best multimodal connection between two places and immediately reserve the transportation space required.

In the course of the completion of service components of the full-service product, further services can be added to the core later. The automobile industry—how can it be any different?—is creating the basis for this: a product platform as a base product and, building on this, value added module components. Two apparently contradictory demands are fulfilled with this concept: the standardization of the core product under consideration of the cost (base product), and the individualization of the extent of service under consideration of the customer (modules). In this, it is irrelevant whether the additional components are done oneself or are acquired from third parties along the lines of a make-or-buy decision.

From Service Provider to Service Broker— Building Network Structures

The problems involved with the make-or-buy decision are drawing more concentric circles around the providers of full-service car management. Full-service management with its individual solutions to problems, along the lines of a seller of a full range of products, will become increasingly difficult in view of the market and competitive situation. However, this is where the opportunities lie for providers. Because of the open architecture of the system, which concentrates on its own core competencies and purchases the supplementary services from strategic partners or finds them for others such as a broker, it is possible to create a meaningful network along the value added chain of a provider, which consists of core products (service and/or administration) and additional products (e.g., financial service, mobility insurance) or vice versa (Fig. 5).

The interfaces to the network partners (e.g., third leasing/financing companies, insurance companies, test organizations) can be designed using business systems adapted to the marketplace. Additional services can be contracted via cooperative agreements or affiliations.

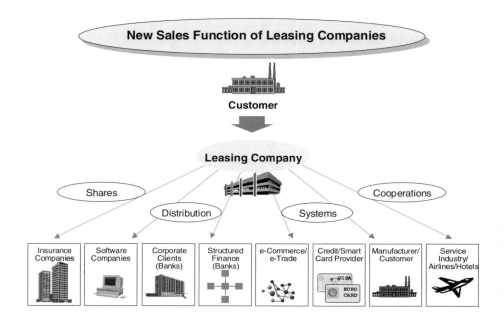

Figure 5 Managing the transfer from service provider to service broker.

Developing an e-Commerce Platform—Building Interactive "Links"

The e-commerce trend is changing the principle behind the business model in full-service car management. Transactions that were done on paper yesterday now are done directly online using PCs and notebooks, and tomorrow these transactions will be handled using wireless mobiles.

The Web will determine the business of tomorrow in full-service car management and fleet management. Cyberlots will cover the entire value chain of full-service car management: from paperless vehicle purchase, through online order tracking and online financing application, to wireless maintenance monitoring and e-trade remarketing/auto brokerage.

Companies such as CarPoint, autobytel.com, or autoconnect.com—the last lists more than 60,000 cars for purchase using color digital photos—are redefining the market. These providers act very quickly and flexibly, and they are creating a new dimension in competition through their activities. This is a development that the major international players in the industry have copied—for example, Ford Credit or GMAC Financial Services.

The right strategy is important for successful entry into e-business. The supplier must decide clearly which path he intends to follow: full-service provider or full-service supermarket or e-trade full service. However, even today, we can foresee that those providers who see themselves as the transformers of the business and whose business philosophy is aimed entirely at customers, resources, in-house capabilities, and state-of-the art technology will be successful, as has already been demonstrated by several failures (Fig. 6).

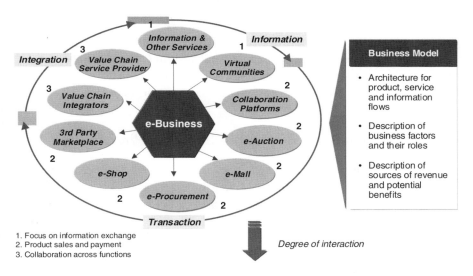

Figure 6   e-business fleet management strategies.

Optimal service in the field of the vehicle will be reflected in more than only the service packages offered to the outside, but also in the provision of internal service and in customer-oriented processes and structures. Thus, for example, a rapid decision on credit financing will be critical for success in competition and is one of the basic attributes of professional providers. Benchmark is an automotive captive which in minutes can decide on individual engagements worldwide. Thoroughgoing "best in class" service at all levels is important, especially when third parties are active in the game. Thus, complete damage claims service and mobility guaranty are not worth much in the case of an accident if the initial information is not taken down completely and the routing to the corresponding service centers or partners does not function well or at all.

Ensuring International Customer Service

"Markets are global, but business is local." This slogan describes the framework in which business operates today and in the future. The creation of providers of full-service car management (including rental) that dominate the market makes this clear: companies such as Ford Credit, Volkswagen Financial Services, or Mercedes-Benz Credit Corp. operate from their headquarters on a worldwide scale with subsidiaries or cooperations/joint ventures. Even the rental industry reflects this. The large American companies have been doing this for some time, and several German companies are following this trend. However, this is not an end in itself. Instead, it is done to follow the customer in his market with service and solutions.

Achieving Advantages in Efficiency—Increasing Profitability

Size alone is not always the decisive factor for a company. A glance beyond the edge of the plate at the equipment leasing industry, in which many vehicle lessors also are active, makes it clear that the healthy path in the middle often leads to better performance. As Arthur D. Little discovered in a worldwide survey of equipment lessors, the most productive companies are often the medium-sized ones and those that stand on the threshold of becoming large. Looking at new business per employee, the companies with a total volume of annual new business of 3 to 7 billion DM ($1.5 to $3.5 billion) have an average new business share of 4.4 million DM ($2.2 million) per employee. Companies with more than 7 billion DM ($3.5 billion) in new business have considerably lower personnel efficiencies due to disproportionate personnel expenses.

This makes it clear that economies of scale can be achieved using targeted organic or strategic growth, which, however, must not be allowed to lead to disproportionate fixed costs in the mid- and back office. It is only the temporary, but considerable, expense of integration of companies that have been taken over or portfolios that cannot be too conservatively planned. The alternative to this, as mentioned elsewhere, is the ability to enter the market and modularize the products using systematic cooperations and/or loose partnerships. Pre-tax return on equity of 20 percent and more is therefore common.

Proactively Challenging Employees— Increasing Knowledge Management

In addition to machines and technology, an important factor is the person. A company lives from its employees, for they make business in its final character possible. Therefore, it is of great importance that employees be proactively selected and trained. However, this assumes that the provider of full-service car management is aware of the customers' demands and how he can fulfill these demands through the selection of his employees at the outset.

The goal must be to fit the employee exactly to the defined pattern of customer demands by adjusting the individual job profile. The important criteria that will increasingly have to be fulfilled by employees in the future are: the attitude of thinking like a consultant, high professionalism, and professional know-how coupled with the ability to innovate and the ability to learn (Fig. 7). Learning and the transfer of knowledge in the company and among partners must be promoted. This is where professional knowledge management becomes more and more important. To actively manage knowledge and to employ it profitably for the company is a core ability. In addition, the adequate use of incentive systems for the long-term motivation of employees is necessary.

The Markets Are Converging

The future will show whether German providers will be able to continue to expand or stabilize their positions. What is certain is that in the future, the market will have to be defined more broadly and internationally, that the pure car business will converge with the light and even the heavy commercial vehicle business, and that the demands of international partnerships will increase for these and other reasons. Learning from each other will take on new dimensions, both within and outside the industry, just as mobility—of data as well as people—is increasing daily. In this field, Germany is certainly a considerable distance from the United States and Great Britain as a site with innovations, but times change.

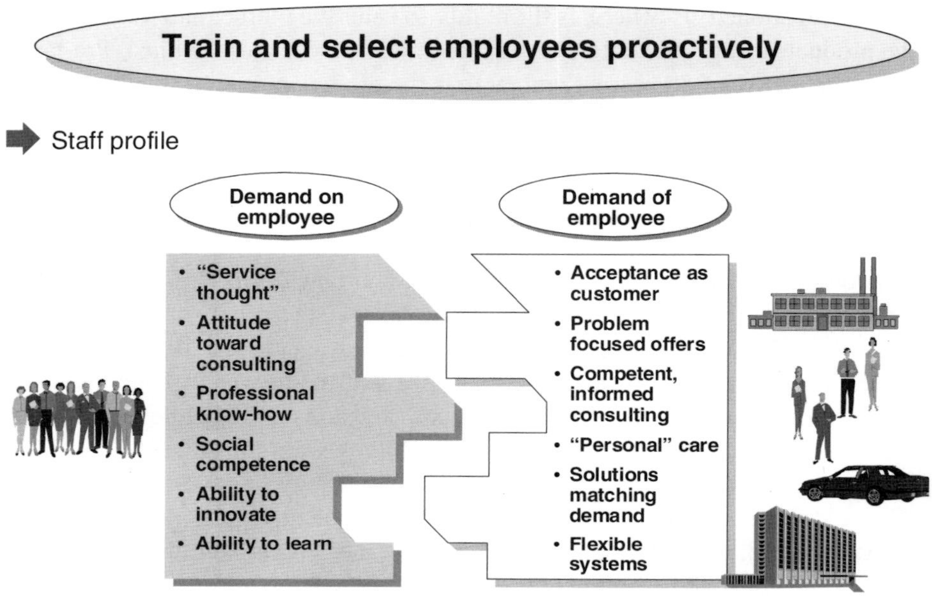

Figure 7   Increasing knowledge management competency.

Case Study:
High-Performance Full-Service Design for Competitiveness

- Offer modular service products designed for the market segment

- Use your own core competencies and combine with the right partners

- Have suitable IT solutions which make workflow easier, make management information available, and foresee electronic links for the customer

These actions were the ones a leading German car fleet management provider that wanted to get ready for competition needed to take. Using the slogan, "High-Performance Full-Service Design for Competitiveness," Arthur D. Little put the provider on the right strategic and organizational track for the turn of the millennium.

To this end, the customer needs in fleet management were first recorded. It was interesting that especially middle-sized service and manufacturing companies with fleet sizes of more than 100 vehicles were looking for alternative fleet financing solutions and saw full-service leasing as an attractive alternative because of their own weak balance sheets and capital coverage. Other reasons also were the desired focus on their own core businesses, the increase in flexibility, service quality of the vehicle fleet, and the use of the more attractive purchase conditions of third parties. On the other hand, for large companies, the reduction in expense was the primary reason that led to the outsourcing of the administrative and technical services. The company-owned connections and means were used for vehicle purchase and financing.

To be able to depict the factors critical for success in the full-service segment, the company's own competencies were critically analyzed in the course of the project. The goal was to identify the gaps in capability in front of the background of their own strengths and weaknesses, to critically examine their previous partnership with a third party, and perhaps to find a more suitable or supplementary partner. The following criteria were significant for the creation of their own profile and that of their partner:

- Strong in sales, marketing, close to customers

- Purchasing power for vehicles and refinancing

- Financial service know-how, depth of the balance sheet, ability to evaluate risks

- Integration of full-service products

- Technical competence

- Remarketing competence with respect to used vehicles

- Functional IT/reporting

- Efficient organization (procedures and processes), critical portfolio depth

In the further course of the project, significant weaknesses were found in the dimensions of financial service know-how, remarketing abilities, and IT systems, which were tackled in a catalog of measures. These included the creation of a short list of possible supplementary partners. The next phase of the project will concentrate on moving the company into a better position in a network with a new legal form and organization, and to influence the incentive and control systems to ensure that the win-win for the partner in any cooperation actually takes place to the benefit of the customer.

Sustainable Development and Mobility—The Challenge for the Motor Industry

Wolfgang Knell

> *The future of the motor car is today one of the*
> *most frequently discussed questions of the age.*
> *No one can ignore this subject or refuse to take notice of it,*
> *as it always concerns the environment and how to sensibly*
> *ensure and plan mobility. This affects us all.*
> —Daimler-Benz (1994)

Only a few subjects are as intensively discussed in association with sustainable development as the effects on the environment created by the current road, rail, and air transport and their future forms. More than almost any other social field, the entire range of the demand for individual mobility on the one hand and for environmental friendliness on the other is reflected in this discussion (Fig. 1).

The high priority in the environmental policy discussion has led to a number of engineering improvements in the motor industry. The introduction of the catalytic converter, the enforcement of higher safety standards, improved management systems, and the presence of a greater proportion of recyclable components in a vehicle are examples of this. Current thrust is directed at alternative forms of power and fuel technologies that use fewer resources. Before it can be shown how the motor industry can fulfill the demand for sustainable transport development, the subjects of mobility and sustainability must be examined more closely. The external costs of transport will then be dealt with before defining the measures that companies can apply to put into practice the philosophy of sustainable development.

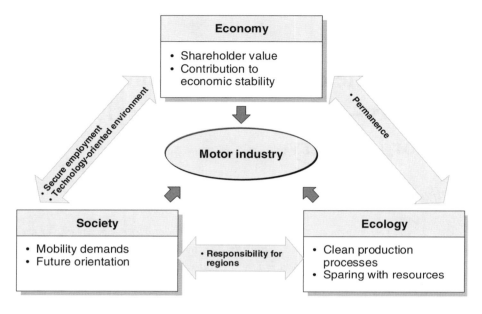

Figure 1   The motor industry is caught among conflicting interests.

More Traffic = More Mobility?

The terms "mobility" and "traffic" were often used in the past as synonyms in this type of discussion. The original meaning of mobility is frequently equated with the number of movements made or the distance traveled. The dynamics of an industrial society are routinely evaluated on the basis of how well developed is its mobility. Increasing goods and passenger traffic is viewed as a pre-condition for growth and prosperity. Mobility currently is spoken of as being the same as transport in all its forms.

The German Committee of Experts on Environmental Issues tackled the definition of the term "mobility" in its report on sustainable development, produced in 1994. It found that mobility should be defined as the ability to move, but not movement as such. More mobility then means more spatial movement options, but not necessarily their use. In Western industrial societies, the concept of mobility often is interpreted narrowly as meaning automotive mobility. The original form of mobility on foot is pushed into the background. This is precisely where the problem of individual transport begins, because if everyone wants to exercise the option of mobility simultaneously, they all will become gridlocked in traffic jams. Figure 2 shows the forecasted development in numbers of vehicles in Germany through the year 2010.

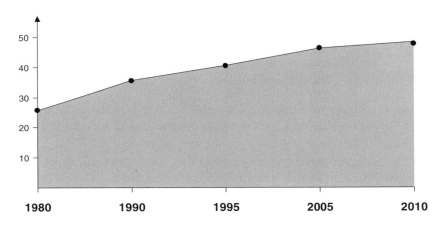

Source: UBA, Nachhaltiges Deutschland, 1997, p. 93

Figure 2   Development in numbers of motor vehicles (cars and estates) in Germany.

This forecast makes it clear that to achieve sustainable development, enormous efforts to reduce consumption must be undertaken. The German Federal Environmental Agency assumes that a pure engineering solution to reducing the carbon dioxide emissions from traffic will not suffice, because the savings would be more than compensated for by traffic growth.

History shows that fast means of transport have a major influence on infrastructure. Schools, shopping centers, and places of employment can be farther away from one another due to currently available means of transport that allow coverage of ever greater distances among them. However, the longer distances make use of alternative means of transport, such as the push bike or walking, less feasible. Free choice of transport mode thus is constricted. Journeys that originally could be made by bike or on foot now require motorized transport because of the increased distances. Groups in society unable to afford this form of mobility thus are disadvantaged, not only by the extant patterns of settlement but by the major spatial demand of the road and rail networks as well. The goal must be to link mobility more with the number of journeys and activities, not only with distance. Even longer distances for an activity do not increase mobility but rather its cost. Here are two simple and convincing examples underlining this:

- Shopping in a nearby store that can be reached by foot is the same activity as traveling using a transport mode to a supermarket farther away—one activity, but two different types of journeys.

- It is almost paradoxical for children to be driven to kindergarten by car because of fears they might otherwise have a road traffic accident.

These examples make it clear that mobility does not mean travel by car. In the past, the automotive industry made strenuous efforts to promote traffic systems solely designed for motorized traffic. Almost all car companies have participated at a European, national, or local level in joint projects and have invested in traffic guidance system research.

Sustainable Development—From Model to Reality

It is no longer in dispute that mobility likewise must subject itself to the criterion of sustainability. The term "sustainability" became globally known in 1987 when the Brundtland Commission on Technology and the Environment presented its report titled "Our Common Future." The concept was interpreted therein to mean that development was to be strived for that complied with the needs of the current generation without endangering the ability of future generations to choose their own lifestyles and to satisfy their own needs.

The approach of the Brundtland Commission does not only cover future generations, but supra-regionality as well (i.e., not only are the needs of future generations included, but also the requirements of countries that are currently underdeveloped) (Fig. 3). It is clear against this background that the lifestyle of the industrialized nations will not be transferable to the entire population of the globe. If one takes account of there being as many vehicles in all of Africa as in one German province alone or that there are as many vehicles registered in a single medium-sized German city as in all of Bangladesh with

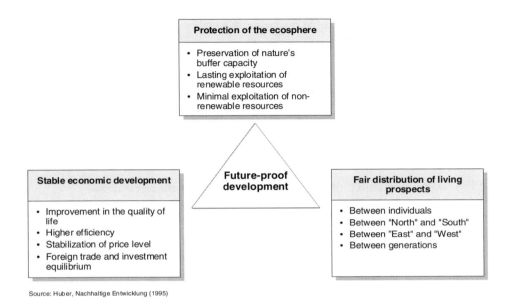

Source: Huber, Nachhaltige Entwicklung (1995)

Figure 3   Future economic goals.

its 120 million inhabitants, it is easy to see the catastrophic consequences of trying to transfer the current standard of Western industrialized countries to developing countries.

Sustainable development has been the cornerstone of environmental policies in recent years. The German federal parliament has set up a committee on this subject, concerning itself with the conditions of any sustainable development. How seriously this is taken politically can be seen in one of the introductory sentences from the report, "On the Road to Sustainable Development in Germany." This sentence states that human life and affairs have reached a point at which there is a risk of our robbing ourselves of our own natural selves.

Everyone involved is well aware that sustainable development cannot be prescribed from above. It will have to be introduced and realized as part of a larger self-organizing process. Thus, the objective of the public sector policies should not be designing the individual processes involved, but modernization of that self-organization. The Brundtland Commission does not reach any clear conclusion in its report on the question of whether economic development or sustainable development should have priority. Five years later, the 178 nations participating in the UNCED Rio Conference in June 1992 took a clearer position on the matter. The final declaration from that conference stated that human affairs and welfare in the classical senses of the words are subject to ecological sustainability. It went on to say that development and hence welfare should be constrained to a level that does not endanger the foundation of all life.

Basic conditions of sustainable development are that the ecological functions

- As the source of renewable and non-renewable resources

- As an absorbent medium of all emissions

- As the foundation of all life

may not be further endangered by exploitation for production and consumption purposes.

The German federal parliamentary commission on "Protection of Humanity and the Environment" has extrapolated four basic guidelines for action from this:

1. Use of a resource may not permanently exceed its regeneration capacity or the rate at which all of its functions can be substituted.

2. Release of materials of all kinds may not permanently exceed the capacity of the environmental media to absorb or assimilate them.

3. Dangers and unjustifiable risks for humanity and the environment due to anthropogenetic effects must be avoided.

4. The time scale of anthropogenetic interference in the environment must be in balanced relationship to the time the environment needs to stabilize itself.

A major challenge is the operationalization of sustainable development. A number of initiatives were taken at the end of the Rio Conference on the basis of the motto "Local Agenda 21—Germany" as guiding principle with the intent of realizing projects on a regional basis. Sustainable development need not mean restrictions on the use of resources. For example, in developing regions, higher contaminant outflow is expected. On the other hand, the industrialized nations will have to realize major reductions in contaminants. Thus, in the context of sustainability, countries of the Southern hemisphere and those of the Northern hemisphere are developing nations.

External Transport Costs

From the standpoint of sustainability, all systems including those of transport must bear the costs of the effects they create. Costs that cannot be allocated to any particular system must be borne by the current or future generations of the general public. Sustainable mobility therefore should cause as few external costs as possible. External costs here are understood to be the negative effects of activities on third parties that do not benefit from the activities. In transport, this means environmental damage and costs for infrastructure which are covered by general tax revenues. That transport causes high external costs is currently undisputed—only the amount is in debate. Cost assumptions range from 2.6 to 36 Pfennigs (1.3 to 18 cents) per person kilometer and from 3.2 to 28.7 Pfennigs (1.6 to 14.3 cents) per ton kilometer for goods. The wide range is due to differences in limits and basic reference data. The income on the other side of the equation from transport-related taxation covers only approximately 50 percent of the costs at the moment. The German Federal Environmental Agency assumes at least 160 billion Marks ($80 billion) in road transport costs. These costs for road traffic are approximately ten times as high as those for rail transport.

Sustainable Development at the Company Level

In the automotive industry, production-related environmental protection and conservation have been at high levels, both nationally and globally, for some time. This industry, taking a cue from the chemical industry, makes sure that national and global standards are followed. This trend has increased in the last four to five years; now virtually all German multinationals in the industry export German environmental standards. Problems arise due to the efforts of other countries to ensure that as high a proportion of all vehicle parts as possible be made locally. The chances of the German automotive industry to influence matters may be reduced by this.

Production-related environmental protection has been extended recently to include

- Product development
- Raw material and components purchasing
- Marketing and customer service
- The recycling of old vehicles

Development of light construction material(s) has become especially important. Weight reduction currently is one of the greatest challenges of the automotive industry. This becomes even clearer if one remembers that 90 percent of the primary energy of approximately 150 megawatt hours is needed for gasoline production (10 percent) and gasoline consumption (90 percent) by a Volkswagen Golf over 10 years of use for a mileage of 150,000 kilometers. The manufacturers look for major weight savings mainly from using aluminum and plastics instead of steel. Bonded materials are also very lightweight and rigid but not as easy to recycle as pure magnesium or aluminum.

Suppliers play a decisive role in the automotive industry. Today, suppliers' product development, production methods, material selection, and purchasing are constantly audited. To influence material selection and processes as early as possible, OEMs in the future will interfere to an even greater extent in suppliers' processes and methods. This is important even from a product liability issue. By the signing of the Voluntary Self-Obligation to environmentally friendly Old Vehicle Recycling under German Recycling Law, the automotive industry agreed to accept the return of old vehicles. Currently, up to 75 percent of an old vehicle can be recycled. By the year 2015, the EU Commission wants this to be 95 percent. In view of the high share of down-cycled material(s) and the expected increase in raw material prices in coming years, the automotive industry has considerable need for research in this field to ensure that recycling laws are met cost effectively. Again, the industry is in the difficult situation of having to produce vehicles as economically and sustainably as possible, while meeting high consumer demands. The flexibility of the industry is further constricted by the many laws and rules that are not confined to only the environmental field.

Alternative Power Sources

Research on this subject is particularly important when evaluating options for sustainable development. All major car makers currently are working intensively on developing technologies that are more energy efficient. This research is concerned, on the one hand, with drive train engineering and, on the other hand, with fuels and their storage (Fig. 4).

Activities	Description	Advantages	Disadvantages
Biodiesel	Choice of biodiesel as fuel	• Exhaust contains up to about 10% less carbon monoxide • Up to 20% less hydrocarbons • Up to about 50% fewer particles and PAKs	• Higher nitrogen oxide and aldehyde values • Reduced performance
Natural gas	Operation of vehicles with compressed natural gas	• Less formation of low-level ozone • Lower emission values	• Reduced range • Increased tank weight and volume
Electricity	Operation of vehicles using electrical power	• Operation without contaminants possible	• Storage problem still unsolved • Reduced range • Emissions caused when the primary energy is first generated
Alcohol (methanol and ethanol)	Operation of vehicles using alcohol from fossil and renewable raw material(s)	• Reduced emission of contaminants • Higher efficiency	• Raw material(s) availability
Hybrid electro-diesel	Combination of at least two power sources	• Exploitation of the advantages of each	• Unfavorable cost/benefit ratio
Fuel cell	Reversal of the electrolysis process to generate energy	• Higher efficiency • Emission-free operation with hydrogen • No energy consumption when idling	• Technically demanding • Long development phases

Source: Umweltbericht Volkswagen AG 1997.

Figure 4   Research into path-breaking motive power technologies stands in the foreground.

Fuel cells are viewed throughout the industry as one of the more promising technologies here. Fuel cells have the following advantages:

- Being independent of the limited resource oil
- Offering high efficiency
- Operating without emissions
- Requiring no energy when idling
- Emitting little noise

Daimler-Benz has been researching this field for many years. Its latest development is the NECAR 3 based on the A Class. This is the first fuel cell vehicle with its own built-in hydrogen generation system. The 38-liter tank of methanol gives a range of up to 400 kilometers. Volkswagen is working on generating hydrogen on the basis of methanol (CH_3OH) using a reformer built into the vehicle.

The generation of methanol is particularly important to developing fuel cells for market. Until now, methanol has been extracted mainly from fossil carbon sources such as natural gas, oil, and coal. This worsens the fuel cell output economics from the standpoint of overall energy benefit. In the future, it is possible that methanol may be generated from carbon dioxide, biomass, waste, or hydrogen using regenerative energy. Sustainability could be achieved using suitable methanol synthesis in closed material(s) cycle(s). This means that carbon dioxide released into the atmosphere after the reforming process could be re-extracted from the air to produce methanol. This form of carbon dioxide recycling could result in a closed loop process that does not contaminate the atmosphere (Fig. 5).

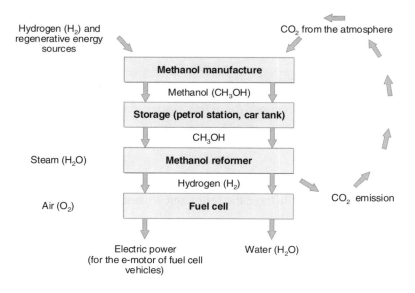

Source: Umweltbericht Volkswagen AG 1997, S. 43

Figure 5   The vision of the CO_2-neutral circulatory process.

The EU is currently subsidizing a project for making fuel cell hybrid vehicles using the methanol reforming process. However, a major problem with this type of vehicle will be the creation of the necessary infrastructure to power the vehicles. Estimates assume that re-equipping every tenth U.S. gasoline station alone would cost approximately 65 billion U.S. dollars. The conversion to a hydrogen network would cost as much as 95 billion U.S. dollars. The Arthur D. Little Technology Center in Cambridge, Massachusetts, together with its European subsidiary Cambridge Consultants, developed a converter that can extract hydrogen from gasoline. This technology makes conversion of gasoline stations unnecessary. The motive power of the vehicle then would consist of a gasoline tank, a converter, fuel cell, battery, and electric motor.

The motor industry is expecting a lot from fuel cell technology research. A big problem here remains the avoidance of carbon dioxide emissions. Only when closed loop processes have been commercialized, and economical methods for mass production of such vehicles are established, will a breakthrough be possible with this technology. Apart from engineering innovations on vehicles themselves, the industry also is working on various traffic management technologies under the banner of Intelligent Transportation Systems (ITS). PROMETHEUS, DRIVE, LISB, and STORM are all projects for managing traffic flow in Europe, while ITS America coordinates the activities in the United States, working with both public and private sectors. Onboard vehicle navigation systems are used to ease traffic flow in conjunction with traffic monitoring systems. This assumes that alternative routes to overloaded roads are available, which is not always the case (e.g., during the rush hour). Improving traffic patterns increases safety and comfort. Noise and emissions can be reduced by improved traffic flow management, and that means environmental relief, at least in part. Economic costs could be greatly reduced by cutting idling times during periods of high traffic load as well.

Car makers also are breaking new ground in system design. Volkswagen has applied a new car-sharing system in Hamburg. Under this concept, the user rents not only a place to stay from a landlord but participation in a car pool as well. The car pool allows the user to select a vehicle appropriate for the journey. In one particular situation, the residents have a total of three Polos, one electric Golf, one Caravelle, bikes, and a city transport annual pass available to them. Even if the overall emission values for any such block of flats are not much lower than in normal cases, at least the idea breaks from the conventional structures. The concept of individual ownership of transport means—the car—is abandoned. That is a good start.

Summary

Sustainable development must be advanced by small, pragmatic steps at the company level. Politically, clear and long-term goals must be set. Everyone involved has the duty to surmount the regional and generational conflicts that inevitably will arise. International organizations such as the United Nations, as well as national or regional environmental organizations, certainly can provide development support, perhaps in the form of technology transfer or making financial aid available as appropriate. They also can create a forum for discussion of industrial development and for defining mutually agreed to targets. Conflicts (e.g., in setting targets) must be identified in good time and openly discussed so that all parties are fully committed to the decisions. At the regional, national, and global levels, sustainable development requires clear definition of goals and decision criteria on which companies can orient their strategies. A poll of 500 European top managers by Arthur D. Little in 1997 regarding what they expect of politicians gave the results shown in Fig. 6.

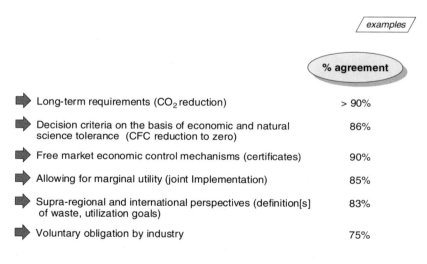

examples

% agreement

Long-term requirements (CO$_2$ reduction)   > 90%

Decision criteria on the basis of economic and natural   86%
science tolerance (CFC reduction to zero)

Free market economic control mechanisms (certificates)   90%

Allowing for marginal utility (joint Implementation)   85%

Supra-regional and international perspectives (definition[s]   83%
of waste, utilization goals)

Voluntary obligation by industry   75%

Source: Arthur D. Little poll 1997

Figure 6 Sustainable development predicates clear political goals and decision criteria.

For more than 95 percent of those polled, the subject of sustainable development plays an important role; approximately 17 percent include sustainable development in their strategies. People are seeking long-term goal setting on a scientifically justifiable basis. Those involved also must show a willingness to enter into a dialog. The sustainability process is designed for the long term. Short-term successes obtained by pulling the rug over problems will not lead to realizing sustainable development. Altruism certainly is a motivation behind creating the policy of sustainability. However, it also could be formed on the basis of enlightened self-interest. Take the example of Germany. The automotive industry is possibly the flagship of the German economy. If it is possible to compensate for the unavoidable resource scarcity with energy-saving technologies, enormous market potential can be tapped. Whoever gets started today on the necessary steps to a sustainable development process, organized on a long-term basis, will reap both economic and ecological benefits tomorrow and the day after tomorrow.

Literature

Daimler-Benz AG, "Daimler-Benz Umweltbericht 1998," Stuttgart.

Daimler-Benz AG, "NECAR 3 mit Methanol in die Zukunft," Stuttgart, 1997.

Huber J., "Nachhaltige Entwicklung—Strategien für eine ökologische und soziale Erdpolitik," Berlin, 1995.

Mercedes-Benz AG, "Umwelt Forum II—Auto und Umwelt, Alternative Antriebe," *Verkehrsmanagement*, Stuttgart, 1994.

Petersen R., and Schallaböck K.-O., "Mobilität für morgen—Chancen einer zukunftsfähigen Verkehrsplolitik," Berlin, 1995.

Stobart R., "Wasserstoff aus Benzin," in *Automobilindustrie*, 7/1998.

Stobbe, R., Volkswagen als Akteur im Agenda 21-Prozeß, Vortragsmanuskript anläßlich eines Hearings der Landtagsfraktion Bündnis 90 / Die Grünen, Braunschweig, 2/1997.

Umweltbundesamt, Nachhaltiges Deutschland—Wege zu einer dauerhaft umweltgerechten Entwicklung, Berlin, 1997.

Volkswagen AG, Umweltbericht 1997, Wolfsburg.

Weizsäcker, E.-U. von, Umweltstandort Deutschland—Argumente gegen die ökologische Phantasielosigkeit, Berlin, 1994.

The Authors
(Selection)

Thomas E. Anderson, Ph.D., M.B.A.
Strategic Business Development

After Dr. Anderson received his Ph.D. in neuroscience from the University of Michigan, he joined the General Motors Research Laboratories to initiate a safety research program focused on brain and spinal cord injury. During his twenty-year career at GM, Dr. Anderson held increasingly responsible positions in research and research management. Most recently, his responsibilities were in the areas of R&D globalization and the development of coordinated global teams for major technology innovation projects. Dr. Anderson also served as the GM representative to the USCAR Joint Support Committee. Subsequent to completion of his M.B.A. through the Executive M.B.A. program at Michigan State University, Dr. Anderson left General Motors in August 1999 to pursue independent business development interests.

e-mail: TEAnderson97@cs.com

Dr.-Ing. Wolfgang Bernhart
Arthur D. Little International, Inc.

Is an associate director in the automotive practice at Arthur D. Little International, Inc. in Wiesbaden, Germany. He specializes in the field of company strategy and structure, knowledge management, organizational development, order processes, and cost improvement. After studying production technology in Karlsruhe, Dr. Bernhart was conferred the degree of doctor on processes of calculation in the stage of development of multiform series production.

e-mail: bernhart.wolfgang@adlittle.com

Marcos Chiorboli
Arthur D. Little Limitida

Is an associate director of Arthur D. Little in São Paulo, Brazil. He is the leader of the Strategy and Resources Industries Practice in Brazil and also a member of the Global Automotive Practice. He specializes in competitive studies, products and manufacturing processes, market structure analyses, market research and entry strategy, strategic positioning of products and businesses, and enterprise restructuring. His professional background comes from 20 years of experience in the leading company of specialty steels in Latin America, where he held several responsible positions. Mr. Chiorboli is a metallurgical engineer from the Universidade Mackenzie and has a degree in business administration from the Fundação Getúlio Vargas and also a degree in industrial administration from the Fundação Vanzolini of the Universidade de São Paulo.

e-mail: chiorboli.marcos@adlittle.com

Jean-Christophe Deslarzes
Alusuisse Schweizerische Aluminium AG

Is since 1998 human resources and administration manager at Alusuisse Swiss Aluminium AG in Switzerland. Besides human resources, he is responsible for the areas of security, health, and environmental infrastructure, as well as public relations. Furthermore, Mr. Deslarzes managed the implementation of empowerment at Alusuisse. Prior to joining Alusuisse in 1994 as personnel manager of the workers, he was a consultant for tax and legal issues at Arthur Anderson AG in Geneva. After his schooldays in Bern and the United States, he completed his studies in law at the University of Fribourg, Switzerland.

e-mail: jean-christophe.deslarzes@alusuisse.com

Andreas Feige
Arthur D. Little International, Inc.

Is a member of the management group of Arthur D. Little in Wiesbaden, Germany, specializing in strategy, technology, and innovation management, as well as in re-engineering. Before joining Arthur D. Little, Mr. Feige first worked in the R&D central department of a large German industrial group. Later, he was responsible for investment planning and automation of one of its subsidiaries. Finally, he assumed the responsibility for project controlling, precalculation, and standardization within a German manufacturer of upper-class vehicles. Mr. Feige received his diploma as a mechanical engineer from the RWTH Aachen and at the Imperial College of Science and Technology in London. He has published numerous articles and speeches.

e-mail: feige.a@adlittle.com

Dr. Holger Karsten
Merrill Lynch Capital Markets Bank Ltd.

Is managing director in the investment banking division of Merrill Lynch and is the responsible relationship manager for key clients in the automotive and transportation industry. Prior to joining Merrill Lynch, he was vice president, member of the German management and director of Arthur D. Little's Global Automotive Practice, with twenty years of business experience. Before entering the consulting industry, Dr. Karsten had been working at a leading German car manufacturer. He studied economics, received his Ph.D. in the area of innovative methods of work structuring, and completed his post-graduate studies at the Business School of Amherst, Massachusetts (U.S.A).

e-mail: holger_karsten@ml.com

Ralf Landmann
Arthur D. Little International, Inc.

Is an associate director (partner) with Arthur D. Little's Global Automotive Practice in Wiesbaden, Germany. Mr. Landmann spent ten years consulting to selected industries worldwide, focusing on strategic planning, marketing/ sales strategies, and large-scale, cross-cultural change initiatives. He began his career with Daimler-Benz (today DaimlerChrysler), after which he joined Schott Glass' (Carl Zeiss) corporate planning/development. Currently, he helps automotive OEMs to launch and grow their electronic- and mobile-commerce strategies. Recently, Mr. Landmann and his team developed a global change-program for more than 70,000 frontline employees, enabling a "Top Three" automotive OEM to achieve behavior in line with the brand with all customer-contact and back-office staff. Mr. Landmann serves on the faculty of the St. Galler Management Program (Switzerland) and is a regular speaker and author on automotive and marketing issues. He graduated with an M.B.A. from the University of Erlangen-Nürnberg, Germany.

e-mail: landmann.ralf@adlittle.com

Dr. Gerrit René Seidel
Arthur D. Little International, Inc.

Is a director of Authur D. Little and gobal manager of the financial institutions practice in the German subsidary of Authur D. Little International, Inc. in Munich/Wiesbaden, Germany. His main activities are in the fields of strategy, organization, and corporate finance. Dr. Seidel studied business administration at the LMU of Munich and completed his Ph.D. (focusing on finance, market-ing). Before joining Arthur D. Little, Dr. Seidel was employed at a financial services company, working mainly on international projects (e.g., Zurich, New York, and Hong Kong).

e-mail: seidel.g@adlittle.com

Dr.-Ing. Tom W.H.A. Sommerlatte
Arthur D. Little International, Inc.

Is chairman of the worldwide consulting activities of Arthur D. Little. He has more than 25 years of experience in assisting and attending companies that have to adapt their strategies and organizations to new requirements in the fields of market competitiveness and technology or intend to develop new opportunities in their business. He was highly engaged in building the management consulting activities of Arthur D. Little in Europe, first as director in the consulting fields of operations management and telematics, and later as a managing director of the European subsidiaries in Germany, Austria, and Switzerland, followed by a managing director's position of all European subsidiaries, and finally as chairman of Arthur D. Little worldwide consultancy activities. Dr. Sommerlatte is the author and editor of numerous books with regard to management issues such as the practice of innovation management, high-performance organizations, and the learning capability of organizations.

e-mail: sommerlatte.t@adlittle.com

Dr. Heiko Wolters
DEKRA Automobil AG

Is director of sales of DEKRA Automobil, the leading automotive service organization in Europe. In this position, he is responsible for controlling and marketing of the more than 200 branches in Germany and is in charge of the key-account management. Before joining DEKRA, Dr. Wolters was a senior manager in the automotive practice of Arthur D. Little International, Inc. in Wiesbaden, Germany. His main activities are concentrated on sales and marketing, restructuring, strategic and organizational development, and productivity improvements. Before joining Arthur D. Little, Dr. Wolters was employed in the purchasing analysis department at BMW in Munich, Germany. After an apprenticeship in banking, business studies in Berlin and Paris, and completion of his Ph.D., Dr. Wolters was a visiting scholar at the Massachusetts Institute of Technology in Cambridge, Massachusetts, within the International Motor Vehicle Program. Dr. Wolters is author of numerous specialized publications, books, and speeches concerning issues of the automotive industry.

e-mail: heiko.wolters@automobil.dekra.de